WALKABOUT RUNABOUT

Richard Chaffer

This book is a work of fiction. Names, characters, descriptions, dialogue and plot, are of the author's imagination and are used fictitiously. Any resemblance to actual events, institutions, intellectual properties, names or persons, either living or dead, is entirely coincidental.

The text of this edition contains revisions and corrections.

Cover design by LeFroste exclusively for EOD by
Giovanni Duenas

Library of Congress
Cataloging-in-Publication Data
Chaffer, Richard
1st ed. U.S. Copyright Office
Copyright No. 1-507875841
EOD California

Printed in the United States of America

To my friends…

You have navigated with raging soul far from the paternal home, passing beyond the sea's double rocks, and you now inhabit a foreign land.

~ Medea ~

One fateful winter, some years ago, I took momentary refuge in a misty cloud of groves to cool my disbelief. Little could I imagine then that such an insidious and terrifying sickness existed. To all that have fallen from the fold, may the powers that be as bravely accept your incomprehension and, occasionally, utter blessings to the lame faculties and the blind eye with which you walk beguiled through heaven.

–R. Chaffer

Part One

I

It was winter and a new year had risen. The rain rattled the window panes and struck sharply at the thin rooftops like great hampers of rice. I sat fidgeting with the piano's keys, trying to learn a new piece, in the streamers of golden candlelight throwing out shadows of memory. My fire, my cave, my ape,' I muttered, stopping my practice to realize the sudden squall knocking things about. The wind gathered, then whistling twice changed, and a branch screeched like a bird against the window. I was reminded, horribly, of the castors on the many hospital beds I had once visited.

Opening the window, I peered strangely out into the stormy night. The quick hands of darkness seemed to reach for me.

The candle's flame stood up like a cobra. In the winds faint sough now something new and rank, fathomless and dreadful, secret and confiding, shrill and frightful sprang up all around me. It was as though I was prematurely awakening from winter's solemn nap. I snapped on a lamp and its light shimmied upon the curtains and across the carpet pleating them with dark folds and sharp edges. The wall mirror, wet with these same oily reflections, released an unsettling chiaroscuro effect upon all objects. I finally leaned to turn off the light, preferring the seduction of the flame.

Though a gray veil of clouds had sat motionless for a few days something vague and restless, normally not found in this murky hail of rain, swam about me. It was as though these live, silver pins tapping above were trying to insistently express something. Of this vibrancy growing throughout the day, crying and kicking from within the swaddling arms of dusk and dawn, I was certainly well aware. And in this backdrop of anxiety and finger snapping a new form was emerging; hideous, barbaric, and criminal. However, a nameless change was happening as well.

All sensation and perception were running their tendrils, sui generis! I awoke to a pale morning feeling light, almost buoyant, and eager for life. My appetite remained healthy but I began to indulge myself in one cup of coffee after another gaining sustenance, vigil, and comfort from the caffeine. Standing to finish some sliced fruit over the kitchen sink, unable to relax in the wake of this newborn energy, I became unsteadily aware of the many sounds emanating from the neighboring walls. Before exiting my apartment I took a peek through the fish eye lens of the door so as to avoid, I would imagine, any confrontation with the very private and quiet tenant directly across from me. After some time of having neither seen nor spoken to one another this evasive practice seemed both mutually and tacitly agreed upon.

Outside the sky had been thoroughly washed by the storm and felt cool, like mint, against my palate. I was in good cheer and recalling music from the night before I chimed, to encourage myself perhaps, 'just like "April in Paris!"

I felt relieved at leaving my bungalow and comforted by a day offering the social interactions of my work at the clinic. Warming up my car I looked around and thought to myself, 'not a soul stirring, not even a mouse!' And then my eyes fastened on a cat on the window sill with the saucer-like eyes of an owl, and I laughed out loud.

It was so very still that I almost began to wonder how long rigor mortis had set in when it suddenly leapt from its perch. The blinds opened at one slat, eye level, then shut. I began to wax antsy and shifted into reverse. As I did so my coffee spilled out into the well of the dash. 'At least that's quite normal,' I thought to myself, as though suspicion was growing hard toward the uncommonplace. Traffic was light yet there was an awkward feeling attaching itself to the spacing of the cars. I looked casually around not wanting to give the impression of directing my attention one way or the other. Then I began to keep a mental record of what was around me and of what became of its course.

Arriving at the clinic I felt something relax and sigh from within as if to say 'safe at last.' However, construction had begun on an additional wing and I was taken somewhat aback by the frenzy of activity. The receptionist nodded a hello with a faint smile. She looked rosy, more resplendent than usual and, with that aquiline nose, appeared all the more the good witch from a fairy tale. She was tolling up yesterday's figures with the adding machine. I stopped to watch her, marveling at the speed of her adeptness. Sounding like the pitter-patter of mice, her fingers pummeled the keys, her bright nail polish gleamed in the humming neon light. The air smelled of rubbing alcohol and camphor. I snapped on the lights, then the ultrasound machine, feeling cozy and befriended in the looming drafts of electricity set loose. After examining my first patient to the blinking screen with rapt attention

I finally turned toward the door with my film headed to the darkroom.

Dating the fetus of my last patient I suddenly began to tire. The obstetrical biometrt trailed into afterimages. Circumferential measurements of fetal heads and abdomens, like so many negatives of an alternating frame rate, danced into the darkened corners of the room. Something was not right! I started to question the ethical propriety of viewing a human life unborn. I felt queasy and bothered by something but I couldn't put my finger on it and so, by dint of habit as much of life is lived, I finally shut off the machine. Anyway, we all have freedom of choice, I heard myself answer as if to console this restlessness.

Returning toward the city through the winding country roads I took notice of the cool apron of the orchards, their shiny green leaves dusted with platinum. The trees were cleft with slim aisles that stood like swathes of freshly cut grass, and there, shadows watered the earth in flickering pools. The plashy grounds of winter's downpour seemed to nudge at spring's christening and in this initiation I was ready for a change of pace, a change of season. As I was entitled to my vacation in the near distance I decided to browse at some brochures at the local travel agency. This should help clear the slate of any uneasy feelings, I reasoned, and awaken memory of more nurturing times.

The sun was now beginning to shine a little warmer and inviting pictures of tropical places floated gently before my eyes. It was a welcome rest from the nervous seed that had been planted in the vague gloom of the past month. A cool swim on a foreign shore soundeduite delicious. To bask in the slower, carefree hospitality south of the border seemed the natural way to go. Neither too far nor too expensive I could almost taste the sweetness of the mango. And I continued to imagine myself beneath the shade of a palm watching the sea gulls frozen still in the eternal light like statuary.

Having soothed myself with these

remembrances I proceeded on in this same vein performing a few lingering, domestic chores and avoiding a quick return home.

Besides, there was ample time before my appointment with the dermatologist this afternoon and I would not have to retrace the distance from home once more. Perhaps after grocery shopping it would be wise to visit a furniture store where I might purchase some reminder of my Asian journey, I reflected. I stopped at a place of business that I knew would house the same affordable bric-a-brac for which I was searching. I was eying a three panel screen of black lacquer and rice paper that struck my fancy when I became engaged in a conversation with a lovely Thai woman whom was, it turned out, related to the owner. We exchanged pleasantries and shortly discussed my visit to her native country. Then I inquired about the curtain that had held my interest, asking her if I might be able to purchase one in cherry wood. She said 'yes' and proceeded to tell me to leave my name and telephone number with her so that her brother might be able to notify me when my order had arrived. I did so, then departing I bade her an affectionate 'thank you' and 'goodbye' in Thai, two of the few expressions I had recalled from my trip. I felt happy momentarily as a fond wave of memory came over me from my time spent abroad. However, as I departed the warm shelter of her company and strolled out into the open parking lot busy with traffic and noise, things began to speed up. Annoyed and suffering some confusion in the bristling traffic, I decided to make haste at the market in order to arrive punctually at the doctor's office. The waiting room was bitter cold. I thumbed through a magazine absent-mindedly. Listening to the giggling and whispering of the doctor's aid behind the receptionist's desk began to rasp my nerves. Soon this obedient mouse called my name. It was time to meet the king of knights, clad in pure white. I followed her to meet this rather stern judge who turned to me to ask solemnly, "what can I do for you?" I explained to him that I had noticed some patches of dry and remarkable nevi and that I was concerned about such carcinomata that ran in the family. But I told him that, as I was presently applying for medical insurance, I didn't want this visit to alter the status of my future coverage by his recording of any problematic sites. Obviously, this would stand then as a pre-existing condition and my insurance would thus restrict my coverage and deny me treatment for a lifetime problem. His arched and furrowed brow prepared me for the chastisement to follow. He lectured to me gravely about the necessity of complete disclosure. He even told me that things had come so far that one had to watch what he said at a party or dinner engagement. "One could never be too careful," he concluded. I simply replied that I was sorry to have taken his time and promptly departed. I arrived at my apartment a little weary and sank down into the sofa; sluggish, bored, and, of course, nervous. The telephone rang frightening me, pulling at me from my well-deserved repose. I did not bother to answer.

After all, what would the other party have to say that could possibly interest me? I was focused on the unnerving sensations pulsing within, infecting the outer world with grave suspicion. The sound was turned down to my answering machine, but I could, nevertheless, see that somebody had left a message. It went through its recording and rewinding functions and the red light began to blink on and off. I managed to stir myself from the gaping silence and, curious about my unheard visitant, played back the recording. The message was simply put, as is the flower of most enamoring. In elementary English, a woman anxiously declared that 'she loved me' and, furthermore, 'that I would see her soon.' She concluded with the interrogative 'O.K.?' And I answered to myself, 'O.K.!' 'For better, or for worse, in sickness and in health,' I beamed with great joy. To tell the truth it seemed like the most natural and honest bidding in my lonely castle to receive such a message. It was a godsend, in fact, though it served only momentarily as a reprieve from the troubles of my day. How long, after all, could one roam discontent; divorced from the stem of life, from the flower of woman? That I didn't recognize her voice didn't bother me in the least. My mind was made up. 'Perhaps an autumn wedding in the Mediterranean, when the fine, evening air has been sumptuously panned like gold and the cool, sapphire sea is as soft as fleece, I delicately proposed. Of course, my secret caller may have been none other than the Thai woman to whom I had spoken at the furniture store. However, in the last analysis, I was unable to match the voice one to the other. It could just as well have been somebody from the apartment complex. I had advertised my car for sale earlier this month and my telephone number had shown in plain view for any acquaintance or stranger to see. 'Mine is not to question,' I exclaimed, still excited by uncertain prospects. I walked casually over to the divan and picking a flower from the vase on the coffee table proceeded to chant, 'she loves me, she loves me not' tearing one petal, then another, as I did so. And I sank into laughter that had, come to think of it, been missing for some time. Though it had the edges of an unusual delirium to it this belly laughter seemed like the merriment of old times and of old humors. Accordingly, I welcomed it with opened arms. 'Why she's probably pilfering the hope chest for the fine linens of our wedding at this very moment,' I shined inwardly. Should all laughter disappear, I thought to myself, even if these are hard times? But I began to take stock of my new feelings, shutting the doors with this return to introspection, on any future bridal plans.Looking around I could see my recent lassitude revealed in the shabby appearance of my apartment. It had become ransacked by neglect. I decided then and there to occupy myself with putting order back into my life. I would spend my day drinking tea and mellowing my mood to some pretty Thai music, sounding like the sweet trek to the heavens from earth. Perhaps, upon recounting my secret beloved I would be able to trim some of the startling exuberance beneath my skin. Yes, I would calm myself by cleaning my flat and doing the laundry to the rhythms I had once known before the advent of this cumbersome load of intuited, small fears and general disagreeableness. With fresh resolve I went about the business of straightening up feeling all the better for it. The day went by rather joyfully, infact, as I strode about humming and whistling, cleaning one room after the other. Life felt promising again accomplishing these simple domestic chores. Yet, how can I describe to you the uneasy feelings that slowly crept into me and continued to spread throughout my day. I not only tidied up, but scoured the entire dwelling with lavish attention. The speed at which I worked never quite appeasing the speed and expectations of my mind. Add to this an unusual sensation in my throat, as though I was being forced to mutter the content of my racing thoughts, and you have the gist of order or disorder in my day. However, I did manage to finally return matters to their normal pace and configuration of mood by rehearsing to myself, in a low voice, 'it will be alright, it will be alright.' As I climbed into bed, my voice box oscillating to the water spinning and gyrating from the plumbing, I beckoned inward with prayer for some saving grace from the powers that be. And with that my body resigned itself to sleep, cradled in the vibrations of background noise. When I awoke I began to recount the dream of early morning. My sleep was becoming more and more dreamless.

Perhaps it would provide a clue to all of this awkwardness. But from within my wakened and alert animal consciousness, I could only recall the sensation of falling. Presently, with both feet firmly planted in the abrupt clamor of reality, my mind had become set like a steel trap, snatching up and collating the slightest noise about me. It was quickly approaching the time for work. I began to rally my resources for the prospects of an unusual day. I felt faint at heart and willing to dissimulate myself in any ingratiating manner so as to stem the tide rising between myself and the uncertain horizon. But with some ambivalence I also felt myself pumping up, acquiring a self image fattening to this new antagonistic order of the day. Assembling my wits with deadly intent, as an army amasses a select arsenal to do its job properly, I steered straight ahead. 'To be able to climb or repel, as the case may be,' I said to myself. With that thought in mind I grabbed the clipboard and a pen from my desk and stealthily left my cool cave buzzing with secret machinations.

The air seemed to render me with a bad case of vertigo; the early, perennial flowers mocking me with their vibrant colors. I walked to my car, head down, yet aware with both my ears and peripheral vision. Starting my car I realized that I had forgotten my coffee laying upon the kitchen table where I was last visited by furtive imaginings. I didn't have the stomach to re-enter that Minotaur's cave and stew, once more, in that anxious setting, let alone permit the possibility of bumping into one of these apparitions boarded up like so many mice. No, I would gladly stop off at a little coffee nook that I knew was placed conveniently on my way to work.

The cat was no longer at the window's ledge nor was there any sign of life next door. Her closed blinds seemed to be shut as tight as the bars of any prison cell. Perhaps my quiet neighbor was ill or dead or suffering from this adversarial force.

However, I lectured to myself, it was an apartment complex; a building riddled with small quarters, separated only by paper thin walls. Privacy, such as it was, exempted me from any responsibility toward both her welfare and her business. Besides, my chief worry and concern was with the woman and two men living on my other side. For it was at this sullen site that I could, from time to time, hear the desperate cries of the woman. Their blinds were opened vertically about one foot high. No life stirred there either though, for one brief moment, I thought that I had caught a glimpse of some motion.

Pulling onto the main thoroughfare I couldn't help but notice the appearance of a car from behind. It seemed to be following me from some deliberate, well-measured distance as a sleuth would follow its prey. 'What we need is a good rat catcher,' I muttered to myself, and I proceeded to take down the license plate number with smug satisfaction. 'No easy prey here,' I countered. But the next thing I knew the car had turned away only to be quickly replaced by another who, likewise, maintained that same stubborn distance. 'A sly game, but played by dilettantes, I assure you,' I exclaimed, rising to the occasion of this heated battle. And I took down his license plate number as well. 'I've plenty of paper here, enough to record the entire city, I beamed, and I continued to write down every license plate within the field of my vision, noting makes and models when able to do so.

Work continued to afford me with some sensible support, taking away the brunt of all of these wearisome patterns of concern. In fact, the importance of my co-workers, the doctor, and particularly, my patients could not be stressed deeply enough. They were of such a comforting power, I must confess, that sometimes I forgot altogether the menace proliferating outside the clinic's walls. It would seem as if there coexisted, side by side, two separate worlds. There was the world of fear and doubt multiplying with every block that I traversed or escalating, moment to moment, in my lonely apartment. This latter world, that is, the world of being alone among strangers signified dread. Then, in puzzling contrast, there was this cozier realm; the world of comraderie and confidence, of private humors and friendship. Here, all threatening signs dissipated into a small corner of my mind. This pardoning reprieve, though quite welcome, seemed to strangely recede with time. Arriving home after a long, harrowing day of work and worry I stepped out of my car shutting off my pager with some finality. I opened my apartment door to let myself in, then closed it firmly, throwing the latch-bolt as reflex. My eyes grazed the telephone scanning for any evidence of messages left. Though no flashing light shone I found myself standing in the middle of the room, frozen in my tracks.

The walls seemed to have a life of their own. They popped and cracked, much like human bones to the adjustment of a chiropractor. Listening very carefully and becoming stillness itself so as not to give away my position, I assumed the age-old posture of predator and prey. I could make out something of a presence, yet nothing was crystal clear. Suddenly the calendar pinned to the neighbor's wall dropped to the floor, it's tack reverberant with a pebble-like resonance that seemed to attack my eardrums with vibrations of fear.

Outside it was dusk, light was surrendering to darkness. I turned halfway around noticing a part of my stethoscope hanging from beneath the blood pressure cuff. I had begun monitoring myself for hypertension and any changes to my vital signs. I felt fear stabbing at me in growing waves. I summoned all the courage I had at my disposal and picked up the stethoscope as one would select an operating instrument. Then I moved to a portion of the wall about ten feet from where the calendar had hung to avoid any detection from the positioning of my eavesdropper. I placed this sensitive membrane of the stethoscope upon the wall as if I was dealing with high explosives.

Finally, it happened! Like the sudden emergence of an intruder toward a child frozen with fear, I discovered confirmation of my every suspicious thought. First there came the acoustics, as of an empty gymnasium, and then, upon the further outskirts of audible range, my enemy. Fluttering like a gnat in the auricle of myear, I could incredulously detect the faint rustling of their presence. I scurried over to another wall and the same tenuous presence was heard. Next, I stood on a chair focusing upon the ceiling. My heart skipped a beat. For even here arose the minutiae of inexact but audible detail that was evidenced upon the other barriers. It could mean only one thing. These vibrations, this soft and idle palaver must be interpreted as an invasion of surveillance no longer limiting itself to vertical borders.

No, these trespassers lay upon my very ceiling as well. And I quickly turned my eyes to the attic entrance. So I was living in a cage, a two-way mirror! I thought. My heart was pounding and my forehead ached. I felt the helpless victim of the meanest of all ploys and pranks. I felt intimidation and discouragement but I couldn't find the strength to further pursue my adversaries by peeping into the attic space. I felt the irritation of a child, as when one mimics another in speech and action thereby repudiating the other. And finally, I felt humbled beyond recognition by this contagion of fear and cowardice germinating from deep within my gut, spreading like bacteria. Thoughts about the guarded words of the doctor resounded in my ears, "one could never be too careful!"

I staggered in this rarefied sense of cognition. The ethereal skein of vibrations was closing in on me. I could almost hear my would-be captors uttering with their thievish and contemptuous snickers. No doubt, they were amusing themselves like a cat with its vulnerable and confused prey. I lit a cigarette and inhaled deeply for some kind of support realizing, at the same time, that I had been smoking more than usual of late. Not a bit surprising, I mused, considering the enormity of circumstance. I took a bottle of cognac from the cupboard. Sitting down cautiously upon the floor in front of the stereo I selected some music that might soften the blow of these new and startling disclosures. I increased the volume to drowned out all evidence of external noise. Lighting a candle in the growing darkness I poured myself a snifter. Downing it with supplications to the heavens above to remedy my situation I looked feebly at the small Buddha icon that I had purchased from my last trip to Asia. Very weakly I smiled at him in his serenity feeling the depth of contrast as I did so. I held on to him noting his smooth, comforting shape in the palm of my hand. Tracing the small facial features I recalled the gentle sweetness of the Thai people. Even though I was not a Buddhist I felt no hypocrisy in keeping his peaceful image near. Especially in these difficult times.

Wasn't my disposition somehow similar? For hadn't I always bent with the river and taken immeasurable refuge from overwhelming worldly cares within this same saffron chrysalis?

After some forty-five minutes of kindlier reminiscence the music and the alcohol began to soothe my anxious self. I went directly to the bedroom and, closing the door for some additional security, fell fast asleep.

The morning light sprang up like the wind, citron yellow. Standing idle in the hallway I reflected upon my situation. It was Wednesday, midweek, or should I say my day of reckoning, I thought, positioning myself with some difficulty into the calendar of routine and daily agenda. The refrigerator stood there, too, humming defiantly. 'This is no time to despair, I am on my own,' I declared with some determination. 'No, one cannot live like this!' 'A night such as last night has to beanswered with positive force,' I concluded.

Whatever surreptitious activity was lurking behind these walls was a violation of my rights, of that I was certain. 'Why, I never before heard of such an unscrupulous preoccupation in all my life,' I exclaimed.

In this connection I rifled through the pages of the telephone book. 'Ah, ivate investigators,' I silently exalted. We would get to the bottom of this answering stealth with more stealth. I had some money saved and an average intelligence. These would surely be the only resources one would need to correct this unsettling atmosphere of events, or so I reasoned. 'One thing at a time, I continued, the main thing is not to panic.' 'I must remain calm as they say.'

Thus counseled, I managed to bring some order and confidence back into my world. Without revealing my hand I would play my cards by enlisting the help of my own anonymous scout. He would be able to furnish me with all I needed to know about the identity of these rascals. In such a way, in fact, that I wouldn't have to openly deal with this opposition in some awkward showdown. In my nervous shock I was not able to count, definitely, upon any sleight of hand nor an adequate poker face. 'No need to expose myself in this quandary,' I further summarized, not a little excited by my own cunning and executive powers.

Though I felt uncertain and somewhat cowardly in acquiring a second party I realized that it was a necessary evil. I huddled into a distant corner of the room, receiver in hand, and spoke in a very, very quiet voice. In measured tones I outlined my position clearly and concisely, sparing the investigator of any fringes of emotion and the telltale signs that were weighing so heavily upon me. In fact, my speech and lucidity illuminated the scenario with what I felt was the exact reserve of judgment on my part. Painting this unblemished canvas of events seemed to help. I neither gave myself up to any of the hysteria of last night nor did I cower from supporting my suspicions with sufficient reasoning, and accordingly, I congratulated myself.

Well, that's done, I sighed. These meddlesome birds won't be a whit wiser to my counterattack. I'll just wait out my time until tomorrow knowing that this case will soon be closed with such decisive dispatch.

II

A part of me ridiculed myself for having made the appointment with the P.I. today at lunchtime. However, I had been so greatly disturbed by the unnaturalness of events lately that I felt it a worthwhile project if it succeeded in dispelling my present fears. After all, if it was executed in adequate secrecy nobody would be the wiser and I would be left holding the trump card, I counseled to myself. Today I'll visit with the P.I. and then, considering the results, perhaps the aid of an attorney. It will all be consummated with the utmost legality and tact and will do nobody any harm, I concluded, bolstering the part of me that hedged at such a plan.

The investigator, a former police officer, arrived punctually at twelve noon. I saw him through the blinds, pulling up in an expensive sports car, directly in front of my bedroom window. Then I heard the doorbell ring. I felt immediately stronger having an ally after the battering my nerves had taken. We exchanged pleasantries in low voices. He inquired as to which neighbor was responsible for my disquiet and I pointed out the direction. He walkedover to the wall and listened for a moment with his ear, staring at the floor in grave silence. Then he walked purposefully to the sliding glass door. Opening it and stepping outside from within the patio's wooden frame enclosure, he stood listening intently upon the neighbors discussing something softly in their patio. It appeared that they were visiting with one or two guests. From what I could gather, standing close behind him, was that the voices seemed to be low and confiding in tone, almost in whispers.

The P.I. stood still for a moment longer then asked where my telephone was located. Again I demurely pointed to its direction feeling perplexed by his question but obediently subordinate to his trained expertise. He began to dismantle the receiver with a final look of some surprise, saying, 'something is not right here.' I hadn't thought that they would have gone so far as to bug the telephone and I grew more anxious. If that was true it would also mean that they had gained entrance into my apartment at some time. I felt a shiver run up my spine.

We agreed that I should call him at exactly ten o'clock tomorrow morning. He was quite emphatic about the time as though it was of some design and special significance. Apparently, by that time, he would have looked into their identities more closely. I would imagine by running a check on their address and vehicle license plate numbers. I had already furnished him with their names which I had collected from their mailbox, along with two of their vehicle plates. We left it at that. I handed him his retainer. His last words resounded in my ears. "They're definitely interested in you!" Before I knew it I was left in the solemn wake of his departure feeling more suspicious than ever. If they had gained access through the attic door they would also have had procured the phone numbers and addresses of family and friends sitting conveniently next to the telephone. As if my own well being was not threatened enough I now found myself worrying about the welfare of others that meant life itself to me. However, I couldn't very well use the telephone to speak of my dilemma nor warn them soon of the risks of danger posed to them. No, I would have to be prudent and use a public telephone tomorrow evening, I suppose, depending upon the conclusions of this private detective, I surmised.

I shut the front door and went over to the dresser drawer where I had stored a string of bells that I had once used as chimes. With quite a jingle and ring I managed to secure them to the inside doorknob of my bedroom. Then I grabbed a hammer from the kitchen utility drawer and placed it underneath the bed. I was taking every precaution now not knowing how far things had gone.I felt enraged but powerless at present and at work I was preoccupied by a growing state of alarm. I had left a pack of matches from just within the front door, noting their exact location with a hair. I also placed entrapments for clues of unlawful entry by both the patio door and beneath the attic entrance. Upon arriving home nothing seemed out of place. For this I was grateful. Could they now be aware that I had found them out and were having second thoughts about their actions? I did not know. I had noticed upon entering the parking lot that their blinds were unaccustomedly closed shut and I couldn't hear anyone stirring about inside nor on the patio. Perhaps they had hot-footed it over to an accomplices after this rare visit of mine, viewing it with some suspicion themselves.

I spent the remainder of the evening with cabin fever, awaiting their return home, thinking of all the fantastic possibilities. Nonetheless, I couldn't attribute to any of this new phenomena a substantial motive. I finally blew out the candle from where I sat cross-legged, like some frightened elf in a fairy tale. While brushing my teeth I noticed something about my appearance that had changed, but I wasn't quite sure what it was. I studied my eyes for some time. They seemed to remind me of the wall hanging portraying an owl that I had purchased a few months ago. It now hung behind me upon the bathroom wall, looking over my shoulder.

It's pupils were greatly dilated and charged with a fantastic alertness. Tired of looking at this metamorphosed self, I finally shut the bedroom door. The bells clanged away like a merchant's shop door at Christmas, giving me a tremendous start. Then I slumped down into bed wishing a resolve to these events.

I awoke feeling refreshed but anxious to get to the bottom of my inquiry with the P.I. At precisely ten o'clock I interrupted my work and closed myself up in the adjoining room to place my call as had been arranged. The investigator answered, all business, and succinctly delivered the news. "These people are being investigated by the drug enforcement agency," he declared with sure knowledge. I asked him quickly about the phone being tapped, sensing some small degree of impatient and haste on his part. He hurriedly negated it and I continued by asking what he would do in my position. He merely told me to bide my time, that everything was being worked out in the strictest confidence and secrecy. I begrudgingly replied 'thank you' and hung up. I went directly to the restroom and washed my face to gain some composure from these unsettling facts.

Upon my departure I noticed a sheriff's car at the emergency room of the hospital across the street. It reminded me of the D.E.A. and I felt myself getting into an unusual state of annoyance at the law for permitting me to move into a sting operation. I selected a few well-chosen curses for him and I began to wonder if the D.E.A. was not mistakenly after me instead.

Perhaps they had counter enlisted the P.I. to puppet this dissimulating report. However, that didn't make any intelligible sense seeing as how I had no record nor dealing with drugs. No, the fellow next door sporting a Mohawk looked like a possible suspect and the woman at his side might very well be a Columbian connection judging from a brief discussion with her some weeks before. Come to think of it, I easily assimilated, wasn't the third tenant unemployed and drove a fancy car. Conceivably he could be the ring-leader assuming a business-like cover not wishing to draw any attention to his shady dealings. In retrospect, I recalled seeing a disposable syringe by the community garbage bin a few mornings ago. At the time I had passed it off as the equipment of a diabetic. Now things began to take on a new meaning.

I thought it best to search for a telephone booth not wanting to lose all circumspection by taking chances with my own phone regardless of the investigator's words. I passed by one, then another, each time they were occupied as if some state of public panic was taking place. By the time I neared my apartment I finally discovered one that was unattended. I dashed over to it to call a friend and inform him of the dreadful circumstances. But by the time I had used my credit card a woman, whom I had once seen at the neighbors, stood by me waiting to use the phone. Well, I couldn't very well speak in confidence with her ears so close by. With good luck the answering machine of my dear friend came on allowing me to say summarily that I had merely called to say hello. I proceeded to hang up the receiver, noticing all the while, the rude impatience of this person next to me. Feeling offbeat about her presence, the P.I.'s conclusions, and the absence of my friend I shot home, eyes glued to the rear view mirror, anxious to relieve my cares with a few laps in the pool.

Climbing out of my car I noticed a policeman cruising the parking lot. 'Yeah,' I moaned to myself, 'don't give up the momentum.' Perhaps the plot was now thickening to include the overt presence of force. 'Why doesn't anyone come out into the light of day,' I questioned. No, instead we replace human communion with drafts of vast dissonance and the clamor of radio and television. The drone, as from orators gagged and talking backwards, fills the air every night and day. There is no getting away from it! When the channel changes you can hear the lucubration of the network priest appealing to the public with weeping violins or the roar of big guns. Good lord, I've had enough of this type of social malaise to last a lifetime. I was aware, as always, of my feelings and perceptions. I knew well enough when I was being visited by unusual circumstances and when I was being possessed. One could never announce any louder the crippling contagion of fear being propagated one to the other. If just one of these players would emerge for a lively discussion. But no, this is the impossible. Instead we sit like moles fussing with our impoverished kingdoms where distance, isolation, and possessions are the warden. Even a small greeting had become rare let alone a smile or conversation.

Did anybody about me seem the least bit

alive? Either at work or walking the streets hadn't the good natured trust and open arms of youth completely disappeared. Why, if it wasn't for my candid, smiling patients I would be entirely without companionship in this modern city.

'But enough is enough,' I protested. 'I will call the D.E.A. and give them a piece of mymind.' 'I know a foul ball when I see one!'

I called the police department to procure the number of the local drug enforcement agency, then I dialed their number, feeling a little awkward as I did so. In the event that my phone was monitored it might be wise, I thought, to ennoble myself with some fictitious prominence in this world thereby creating some anxiety in the heart of my opponent. Accordingly, while waiting for the rude receptionist to connect me with one of the hired guns, I mumbled, as if speaking to somebody in the room, 'yes, as a young man I had worked for military intelligence, a contradiction in terms, and I know how these matters are both hatched and dispersed,' and I stifled a laugh excited by my own wicked thoughtfulness.

'Yes,' growled a tired man from the other end. I gave to him an invented name and proceeded to explain my situation, thus tempting his curiosity if he already knew who I really was and of my dilemma. It was time to mix things up and to obscure my identity for the sake of confusing them all. Naturally, it was important that I lead these lions along with some form subterfuge without permitting them to come for my blood. I explained my feelings of resentment for risking my life in this cat and mouse game that they were playing at such proximity. He asked me how I knew that the D.E.A. was near. I told him that the P.I. had told me, thank goodness. The manon the other end, clearly incapable of regret and with the voice of a coroner, proceeded to tell me that it was impossible to know and that he never heard of me. I promptly hung up, not only tired of this growling bear, but realizing too that my time to avoid a trace was up. Well, I have met some cold fish in my time,

I muttered, but this one takes first, second, and third place. Anybody can play the taciturn Socrates, but to what end?

I sat sleepily transfixed and in my beleaguered mind I began to review the principle details from my arrival here to the present. I recalled the first time that I had been shown the apartment. I had come across a pipe for smoking marijuana. It was lying upon the kitchen sink, probably left there by its absent-minded owner. The manager and I both hesitated, then laughed for a moment over its presence. I never had anything against the use of marijuana but didn't use it myself not enjoying the way it affected my senses with an instant and giddy stupor. Come to think of it, this former occupant had subscribed to a weapons publication. I knew this much from having received some of his mail that had not been properly forwarded. Was he, perhaps, mixed up in some foul play? I wondered.

Furthermore, I remembered the eerie stillness of the entire complex the day I had moved in. Absolute and impending, the shock of this silence dusted every surface. I also recalled my asking for help to move a sofa. Help that was denied me very coolly, I might add, by some nondescript, middle-aged man. Normal enough, I had thought at the time. After all, the modern apartment was not well known as a place for hospitable lodgers nor charitable acts of kindness. However, now I began to associate his indifference from my present vantage point. It began to look more and more as if it was possible that I had been singled out from the very beginning. Nobody here, but the manager, was the least bit amicable. No, not in the beginning, certainly not now, not in the parking lots or laundry room, and not at the swimming pool in this recent lovely weather where I typically took a swim alone.

As I say, these were only vague remembrances and observations undeserving alone of any concern. Yet when pulled into the greater picture, forming with both time and facticity, they seemed to beg for reflection. Yes, it was as if each memory formed a step to understanding the moment, an integer to add summarily to the daily account of business at hand. And that business for me was to, if necessary, ruthlessly seek out the source responsible for changing and interrupting the natural ebb and flow of thought. 'Forget about it,' I would often hear myself say. Then, as if something gripped at me from beneath all appearances, I would be hurled once again into a form of opposition, my senses indignantly and waspishly buzzing with attentiveness.

III

The minutes and hours ticked slowly by. A few days limped past. One week folded over into a new month bearing numberless imaginings. I began to feel abandoned by all in my pursuit and this grave mutiny started to color the complexion of all plans and preparations for my future.

Sleep was becoming more difficult. My mind raced along eager to perform in this vast theater. Meanwhile, I had invented a game. I would ask myself questions from a range of subjects I'd once studied in school. This served a double purpose. On the one hand it acted as a test of my memory. On the other it allowed me to channel all of this raging mental flux. If the subject had an evolving chronology I would then try to reproduce all of the coeval ideas and discoveries, in a comparative flight of fancy. All answers were acceptable! Why stop the flow to this wild exuberance, spoiling my game for the sake of tedious tradition, I reasoned. What I didn't know I would invent with diabolical ease. Sometimes I would laugh out loud at the new history of these disciplines being laid.

Occasionally I would hear popping noises and I would quickly search for any fresh cracks in the plaster and drywall. I would often wonder what the neighbors were up to. Looking around at the disarray of my apartment I would reflect upon the inertia that went, hand in hand, with this blistering anxiety. I needed to take some air. As disturbing as it might be, I decided to mingle with the public before work.

"Yes, a coffee house,' I resolved, more out of habituation than interest.It was now early spring. New signs of life had begun to appear. An immense stillness seemed to have spread over the land. It was a haunting, reeling silence so deaf-deep one could hear the dead roar.

Yes, it was so quiet you could hear the grass grow, as the saying goes. The crisping of my leather jacket sounded a little like a creaking ship, salting this mortal wound of perception. Mustard stained the emerald fields with the sunny essence of light.

Puddles lay like mirrors for playing children. Ecstatic crickets prematurely chirped to invisible stars, ushering them to wink brightly with sweet song. Everything was pricked with excitement. You could almost feel the motion of the earth, register the body's smooth Circadian rhythms.

Even the morning's water tap precipitated memory and sounded like a thousand seething freshets.

I could see two separate parties sitting in the coffee house. While a car was pulling in from behind me, another headed toward me from the other entranceway. 'Damned, if this thing isn't of colossal proportions,' I moaned. 'Surely it is time to seek some additional help. Better, after all, to spend a dollar today and put an end to this unbridled harassment,' I concluded.

I walked gingerly to the phone booth which had just been deserted by a mother and her child. I took a piece of paper from my wallet upon which I had written the name of a law firm that I had passed some few days ago. The telephone book was missing and I didn't have the patience to search one out. I cupped the paper in my hand so that no passers-by could read it and discovered through information the number of Mr. Paul Ivy, attorney at law. Shortly, with a soft voice, I was able to obtain a free consultation appointment with this prosecutor. I sauntered happily to the coffee counter, my spirits renewed. The counter person smiled with what seemed like complicity. She put the finishing touches on my order, frothing the milk, and humming aloud. She licked at her upper lip with a little cat-like tongue. Cute as a button, I thought to myself, and happy with her work. But why shouldn't she be in such warm and sociable surroundings. And I began to think about how nice it would be to own a cozy café, making espresso and Italian sodas for my sleepy cliental. However, my reverie was interrupted by the sound of an ambulance. Back to work, I lamented, again feeling hemmed in at this reminder of my profession.The coffee comforted me but former light-hearted memories of morning kisses, the soapy smell of a woman's neck, and the garden variety of oils in her hair disturbed me greatly. It was, after all, such a startling contrast to the lonely climate of doom that I was experiencing now on a daily basis. After work I hopped into my car pleased to be done with it and headed toward home watching the sky and fields surrounding me. The sword of the sun would flash or sat still, glimmering like a diamond. At this time the center of things seemed nowhere, yet it was everywhere and the anxiety was blinding. Everything was draped in the brilliant cellophane of its colors. This luminous sheen, this empty rind of costume jewelry coated everything bequeathing an illusory appearance. I was reminded of Plato. However, in a more forgiving shade every evening it would fall to the horizon the color of an apricot. Then, before this twilight of darkness, the dusk would wave its violets and something within me would sigh. For it was at such a time that this midnight-blue shadow, like the presence of Morpheus, would befriend my nerves and the protean variety of the day would subside.

Arriving home from work I cautiously opened the apartment door, careful not to disturb my markers. Noting that they had not changed I looked, from habit, toward the answering machine. The light was blinking and I moved curiously toward it to retrieve my message.

"We're going to kill you; cut you, your dog, and your whole family up good," the caller declared with a Spanish accent. Next, a woman, with the same matter-of-fact voice, issued the same idiotic threat in elementary English. Is this the small potatoes I'm dealing with, I thought with some amazement. And I began to reel ecstatically, thanking them for being so foolish as to leave a message that could act as voice identifying evidence. What nitwits and lowbrows, what reprobates, this infested family, I cursed. I began to implore theatrically and loudly enough for any attentive ears to hear; please don't kill me, nor my invisible dog, nor my imaginary family.

No, these people were incapable of doing the least bit of homework. Had theymade the slightest efforts of inquiry or simple observation they would have learned their mistakes. I laughed and gurgled now excitedly. Feeling that I had the upper hand against a bunch of flunkies, I continued to parade them with intimidation for all to hear, smearing their cowardice and stupidity in their own faces with a relish. 'Stilettos or hammers,' I mocked brazenly. I was finally feeling some definition of human contour returning to the frighteningly wispy, nameless phenomena that went before.

The rest of the evening passed by uneventful enough. The neighbors had returned home around eight o'clock, but seemed quieter than usual. My head was buzzing with ideas as I tried, unsuccessfully, to place all of these characters in their respective roles of 'good guys' or 'bad guys', so to speak. I had decided by now to go through with my appointment with the attorney tomorrow feeling more than a little transgressed by both parties.

At least I'm getting the facts straight, I thought, placing myself within the confines of this new equation. One never knows what is going on in the honeycomb of activity that is an apartment complex. It is only the lonely stage wherein all of these silent and indifferent strangers gather to anonymously share every amenity, locked up within their cells.

Well, I was making some progress, though the findings had become a little disturbing. And I suspired, brushing my fingers along the smooth edge of my hammer beneath the bed, turning my face to the pillow in sleepy resignation.

My attorney sat, hands folded upon the desk, giving himself up to the details I was recounting to him of my ordeal. I continued on using both discretion and only some few words to illustrate the matter. I outlined the minor clues of surrounding noise, the telephone threat, and the private investigator's conclusions. We were shortly interrupted by the ring of the telephone.

The lawyer answered with a simple 'yes,' then 'no,' and his eyes fixed themselves upon me momentarily. Finally, as though aborting the conversation, he intoned 'goodbye.' Hanging up the receiver he turned toward me and nodded, shutting his eyes for a brief moment, collecting his thoughts with what appeared to be some difficulty. Then he proceeded to tell me about the artful game of surveillance, confessing that he had once worked for naval intelligence during his stint in the armed services. I became a little surprised, wondering if this was an allusion to my fictitious ploy practiced recently when I had mentioned in the backdrop to the D.E.A. that I had worked, at one time, for military intelligence myself.

He seemed to brighten considerably as he elaborated upon the play permissible in such a volley of intentions. To illustrate his point he described an incident wherein the U.S. and Soviet intelligence would send Christmas greetings knowing one was listening to the other. However, myattention began to transfer itself to a car pulling up into the parking lot. It was framed by the window just above my lawyer's head. Then I heard him say something about keeping a daily diary for future record. As he stood, so did I, reaching our hands out to shake in mutual confidence over these matters. It was decided that there was nothing that I could do as of yet but spar away my time with this sporting 'give and take' attitude. It was a ploy of trust, I suppose, like the kind developed between victims and their captors.

This advice would have to satisfy me for the meantime, I gathered, though I was somewhat put off from having lost the sanctity and refuge that was once my home. I certainly had it in me to collect my wits now that a third party had been introduced to the nature of my situation. By rising to the occasion I might even find it an inventive past-time, tilting the scales of persecution, so to speak. There, that feels better, I heard myself stammer in self congratulations again. It never hurts to inform others better adapted to such goings-on.

Yes, this attorney was a sly bird, to be sure. If the intrusion became illegal I was now well-prepared, I thought, not without a little gleam in my eye. However, as soon as I stepped out from the shade of the main building, the sun glaring into my face, I began to feel mixed emotions and the exacerbation of an old mood.

The cars and traffic all about me seemed to have faded and there was a dead stillness to the air. I saw the car that I had observed earlier through the attorney's window drive solemnly by me.

Whatever my visit here had accomplished, I now realized, was certainly to further infuriate some of these dawdling eyes about me. I began to feel alone again and to prepare myself for a lonely night of battle.

I pulled out into the street feeling more and more trapped. Traffic suddenly seemed to be lurching carelessly around me. Something that goes well with this type of anxiety, I thought to myself, and I made a right turn into the supermarket. I strode down the shiny lane, brimming with cans and boxes of bright labels staring out at me, toward the multicolored bottles of bold and terrene vintage. Some old world remedy for these new world affairs, I muttered, feeling a little sheepish for having to consult this form of refuge. A barbecue and some fine wine to drive away these ghosts, demons, and hobgoblins, I retorted with joy. Perhaps something of a divine and arid must, vibrating the palette with the cymbal of light and rain, trampled upon by peasant feet and blessed with nature's raised skirt.

While purchasing my goods at the counter an angelic child looked up at me smiling and beaming with joy. "Hi," she said with great curiosity, and continued on dreamily in sing-song fashion, "what is your name?"

I answered, somehow deeply touched and hurt, then asked her the same. "Amy" she answered swiftly and certainly, as if there was only one Amy in the world. And I smiled with paternal sentiment, feeling a tear well up from deep inside me over the contrast of her beautiful innocence with my deplorable situation. "B-bye sweetheart," I softly said with a brief smile, feeling like a fugitive and ashamed at not having a family of my own.

Thank goodness for her smile, I thought. It will surely be enough to erase my cares for the remainder of this restless day. I turned on the car radio to dissuade my attention from the jarring traffic and noise swirling about me like a swarm of mosquitoes drawing blood from my brain.

A sweet, adolescent tune was playing and I began to count my blessings realizing that there was a light at the end of this darkness. That I could always move to a new location was a brightening possibility. But, all of a sudden, something happened! For just one split second, no more, I thought that I heard the word whispered ever so lightly 'amazing.' I immediately reached to turn down the radio. No, upon waiting, nothing else followed. I turned quickly to glance at the back seat for some assurance and then at my friend, the clipboard. It was filled with license plate numbers bringing me back to my senses. I looked into the rearview mirror. A police car was now close behind me following at an even pace. All other cars that had been speeding passed me presently lined up in tow, getting in sink with the rhythms of the law. Well at least he is on my side, I thought to myself, wishing that I was already home and away from all of this obvious attention. I noticed the flashing of lights in my mirror and I pulled over anxious to confront a new possible source of information. But the police car zoomed passed, lights ablaze. 'Go get him,' I cheered, wondering all the while what it might have to do with me. Soon I pulled into the apartment complex thinking of only one thing-a swim.

The exercise gave to me some relief from

this choking collar of reality. I seemed to find myself swimming exclusively underwater which was different. At first I attributed this to a healthy curiosity about my lung capacity, holding my breath as I did when I was younger. However, as well,

I took simple notice of how good it felt to become a part of this other element. Free of gravity and disappearing from all seeing eyes, I coursed the pool as if it was a stream to the sea. For a brief respite, at least, I was able to extricate myself from beneath this dome of gloom, from within this burgeoning species of fear.However, inside my flat the noises continued to haunt me. Everywhere that I went seemed to be answered by similar footsteps on the opposite side of the wall. In a mirror of noise every gesture of mine as now peculiarly echoed by the neighbors; the shutting of a cupboard, running the faucet, closing the refrigerator door, or flushing the toilet. What I needed, I realized, was to speak in confidence with a friend. What I didn't need was to endanger him in my folly and predicament, whatever its contents might be. I hurried to dress and left to find a public phone, composing all the while an adequate description of what was and had been taking place in my life. With this preparation I hoped to appear clear and singularly minded, as when an attorney makes his appeal to the jury. I wished only to stray from any of my weaker suppositions, bringing both clarity and direction to my alarm. Yet I didn't want to startle nor disturb my friend's peace of mind. No, I would play it conservatively and, by staying in the middle of the road, avoid both panic and isolation at the same time.

It was difficult in my confusion, I admit organizing my thoughts to communicate this problem with the proper poise and in a justifiable light. However, after some time passed, I managed to get a grasp of the essential details and I dialed the number. 'Make it plausible and palatable,' I reminded myself. I was struck, you see, by the lingering sensation of having been dismissed with some inattention the day before. Perhaps my co-workers had been simply too busy or, more likely, too typically disinterested when I had outlined my situation for their judgment.

I stood there, jiggling the coins in my pocket with some nervousness. Eternities seemed to pass before me, my mind wondering into abstraction. 'God, he is home,' I mumbled, and I finally relaxed as I heard his greeting voice. I began with the usual pleasantries and then eased into some of the more salient features constituting my fears. But it was so reassuring hearing his voice that I nearly forgot my unusual situation altogether. In fact, surprising myself, I seemed to make light of the entire affair. No need to infuse him with worry, I thought to myself. After all, donning this mask of good humor was the brave thing to do.

Walking back to my car I felt, at once, lonely again and harassed by the increasing noise of traffic. Engines were digging into themselves with such violence while others sputtered out in the sorrowful distance. The sound of rubber on pavement, of horns honking, and of auto alarms being set off jangled my nerves.

Instinctively I wandered back to the phone booth. Dialing the number of another friend, I was finally greeted by an answering machine. I felt desperately disappointed and now felt like talking to anybody, the operator, anyone would do. I dialed still another friend and very thankfully found him home. By this time, what with the traffic and the brunt of my loneliness, I began to lose some of my former composure. I now dug into the subject of my worries with wild abandon.

Telling my poor, unfortunate friend one detail after the other, I unloaded my burden with babbling speed. A car pulled up, its driver waiting to use the phone.

Meanwhile, my friend began to question, and so as it seemed to doubt the veracity of some of my claims. I felt like an innocent man on trial without any supportive evidence on his behalf but for his innate senses and reasoning. Consequently I began to flounder in my own trepidation. Thus I stood in the refrain of our conversation, silently recalling the many horrible days and nights in exquisite detail. He even went so far as to ask if I was taking any drugs. When I vehemently protested he said that perhaps I should see somebody, a psychiatrist or counselor. I succumbed to him with obliging courtesy, not being able to get off the phone quickly enough. So much for diplomacy, I declared to myself, thinking about what a rambling fool I had been. Yet I felt my credibility somewhat sacrificed by his suggestion. Was it possible that 'they' had gotten to him? Had he, too, been muzzled and put in the stable with the rest of these bleating sheep? On the other hand, I thought as I reclined into my car, was my dear friend trying to tell me something more. Why, it wasn't too far fetched to presume, with his noble wit, that something such as a secret rendezvous might very well be his innuendo. Once again the order of things dictated stern measures and I exclaimed, 'damn, if this thing isn't bigger than an elephant.' 'Calm down,' I reminded myself. It was a long shot but if both parties were listening in wasn't this clandestine approach the only recourse? Insights into the lecture given me by my attorney began to dawn on me with new meaning. By chance he, too, may have been trying to signify the breadth and depth of my troubles. Another thing, I said to myself, scrutinizing the raw datum of our exchanges. Hadn't I been jarred a little by my attorney's reference to having served in naval intelligence? Had he somehow been privy to my theatrics the other day? After all, I had invented this same vocation as a former military intelligence servant. Was he thus relating to me by some distant means? Filled with nausea I turned slowly toward the phone. It was occupied by some shady looking character. Was he attempting to retrieve from the operator the phone number last called by some deception and for his own spurious reasons? 'Nothing but more unanswered questions,' I sighed. Speeding down the road I began to stew over such possibilities and the jeopardy in which I had hereby placed my dear friend. Yes, I confidently agreed, I would pursue his lead. Friendship is friendship and he wouldn't lead me astray.

IV

The next morning I stared dumbly at the telephone book. Picking my way through the pages I wasn't quite sure how to select the analyst secretly awaiting me. It was of some necessity that it be a woman. For I would certainly find it more effortless in the recitation of my story. But which one, I thought with some confusion. I decided upon the doctor with the loveliest name and proceeded to call. I was, oddly enough, able to make an appointment with her that very same afternoon. Having no receptionist she answered the telephone herself and after summarizing my situation she consented. 'Well, she sounds delighted to see me,' I beamed. Perhaps she was well informed beforehand or a wire tap had been placed and I was simply speaking to some awaiting impostor. Such a deceitful intercession would be the most convenient way to make things right. Come to think of it, wasn't it strange that she had no receptionist and could visit with me so soon? I wondered. Possibly through some contrived delay she had become informed by this agency. It had rung, I now recalled, for some time before she answered. I could only hope that if she had become introduced to my dismal state of affairs it was without any misgivings. In such a diplomatic way, in fact, that I might kiss the gentle hand of altruism and spare myself the sequestered blows of these specious demons, who were quite appropriately summoned, like the devil, without announcement.

I needed to leave my abode. It was a bright day and, even though considerably warm for morning, I still desired a thoughtful cup of coffee. I drove to the familiar haunt of my coffee shop. The many customers chatted away, idly dreamed, or gobbled up the latest paperback. As had now become quite common, not a soul glanced my way. Apparently, this danger had come to infect us all. I made my purchase and retreated to my car for a private consultation of my own. Drinking my coffee I began to arrive at a new tact. There were so many angles and this was all so very unfamiliar to me. After all, vigilance and delirium had become my best friends. Henceforth, I decided to balance myself by reviewing every possible aspect of perception. For instance, I began to postulate, nudged by the familiar smell of coffee like an old, conniving chum. I would be best served by not only hearing what this therapist has to offer but by making manifest my own observations for the record, so to speak. I would thereby leave a trail to all pertinent parties that would be undeniable should there be any shady intentions or a future inquest of sorts. 'Cover all bases, lad,' I heard myself say with embracement. This will certainly give you the edge!

In this train of thought I raced to the police station risking what there was to risk. Above all, I couldn't be blamed for wanting to expand my own market of acquaintances and, by going somewhat public, saving my own skin in the process.

In what was becoming a rather tedious and redundant script I told the policeman of my ordeal in a forthright and succinct manner. I was, of course, in no mood to parley nor be easily dismissed. Gazing at me dutifully and with some impatience, as the P.I. had once assumed, he insisted that was the way the D.E.A. operated. A sadistic smile seemed to wander across his face as he self- righteously asked "what do you want me to do about it?" I merely protested the authority of the D.E.A. explaining that in a world where one's own well being was so easily dismissed was no world at all. But my little tirade fell upon deaf ears and I soon scrambled to my car, exasperated by his method of dismissal.

Tapping at the steering wheel I sat biding my time until my appointment with the psychiatrist. Occasionally, my eyes brushed against the gray cover of this cell housing our public servants. After approximately twenty minutes had passed I was finally ready to depart for this curious meeting. I started the car, my eyes focused upon the intersection in front of me. What appeared to be the neighbor's car slowly drove by. Could they now be thinking that I worked for the police or D.E.A. and against them, I wondered. They must have seen me wearing a pager before and might have been suspicious from the day I moved in. If they were inclined to suspect me now all doubt had been removed. I spat outside the window in disgust over the indifference of the police and at my blunder for having come here in the first place. 'Oh, well, I'll probably have hell to pay tonight,' I thought, dreading my trip home.

I felt some apprehension with this travesty of visiting a psychiatrist. However, why not, I questioned, let's see how far we can all take this. Maybe I have lost my senses, I pondered with some reticence. At least she may be a messenger of some sort providing a clue to this mayhem.

Hounded by the wind whistling through the cracked window, I drove to the address by the directions given me. For some reason, indecision perhaps, I was having more trouble than usual following them. I entered a square garden setting formed by the surrounding offices. Some, I noticed, were occupied by accountants, others by architects, and still others by various consulting firms. All in all, this mixed batch of businesses seemed odd of itself. I was used to such buildings being exclusively medical in nature and I balked at this heterogeneity with some surprise. Was this an elaborate sting operation? I queried. None of these professions seemed to present themselves as very permanent or enduring practices. In fact, it looked as though they had all blown in with the last prevailing wind. Their anterooms were generally quite barren and papers were strewn over their desktops in disorder. But the garden fountains lapping at my ears and the cool, breathing greenery, for the moment, soothed my leaping nerves.

I moved hesitantly toward the columnar chute in the center of this court that housed the elevator. As I approached the doors opened suddenly and out strolled a woman. After looking me up and down she asked if I was so and so. Yes, I affirmed with a faltering voice and I looked her up and down. She hastily explained that she would be back momentarily and that I should take a seat in the waiting room, second floor, suite 221. Soon she was walking away and the elevator doors were shutting automatically before me as if by some invisible hand.Suite 221, eh! Another coincidence, I thought to myself. For this was the street address where I had lived as a child and consequently I shuddered. Wasn't it both rude and curious that she hadn't shaken my hand? "Curiouser and curiouser" I sang to myself, feeling a little bit like Alice in Wonderland. Well, any fool could see that such a personable atmosphere of confidences and trust easily requires the rudiments of politeness that she had forgotten. And then, of course, why had she left and where was she going-to make secret preparations perhaps? I began to imagine her briefing a couple of men with their shirtsleeves rolled up, tending to their electronic gear. All of these considerations were slowly sinking in, turning me a little gray with alarm. The waiting room was deathly empty and there was no receptionist in sight. It looked as though the room had been set up in a hurry. One picture adorned the walls, a Monet, I believe. A few of the typical array of magazine publications lay upon a Formica table. A source, no doubt, of simple diversion from real life where the glut of gossip never ends. I sat down staring blankly at this disheveled pile of literature tossed about to give this sterile room that 'lived in' look.

After waiting for what seemed to be an eternity this princess of impropriety showed up. I moved, at her bidding, into her confidential quarters and took a seat. She still hadn't greeted me officially nor respectfully and I felt, at once, far removed from her. No, I didn't like her from the very beginning. I abhor sloppy manners.

So this was the modern day priest, no more

than a cog in this fast moving world. Her distance seemed a little too affected for my taste. She was beginning to give me goose pimples from the coldness she emitted. I had originally chosen a woman psychiatrist for the reason, as I have said, that I am morenaturally inclined to share openly within their warmth and tenderness. This contrast was unsettling to say the least. She began with the usual questions and reminded me grimly of the inhuman, starched shirt at the police station. I very briefly reviewed my present situation sick to death of recounting it. Why, if she isn't playacting, the little dickens, this evil stepmother and tonsorial witch, I sneered. She simply has never met one so practiced in methodical doubt and sophistry, I surmised, not being able to accept her feigned character. No, what she needs is a few more dress rehearsals before meeting the likes of me. And as she began her inquisition I slumped down in my chair feeling small and growing smaller, as docile as a puppet.

"Do you feel as if people are controlling

you?" she asked. I snickered, instead of telling her what she probably already knew-that they were, I answered 'no' very demurely. I knew that these were questions asked to determine schizophrenia and I began to anticipate the inquiry to follow, answering her cautiously and equivocally so that I neither committed myself to a 'yes' or a 'no.' 'Hmm!' The doctor was probably involved, too, and there was no telling to what lengths this organization would go to entrap me.

Besides, I was fearful of what they might be concocting for me in the adjoining surveillance rooms. After all, I still didn't know who to believe or the nature of these forces at work. What might I be playing into but a final trip to the sanitarium of my choice!

She proceeded to ask me, "who is the governor?" For some reason, to break the monotony of this cuckoo chase perhaps, I responded immediately with the name of a well-known comedian. Meanwhile she quietly laughed and I, I corrected myself with the appropriate reply. That a boy, Bimbo, I insulted myself to encourage this triumph of having provoked a response outside of protocol. Accordingly, I readied myself. "Who is the president?" she resumed. Puzzling for a moment and wiggling in my chair with hesitancy I finally rattled off a revered musician with a boyish grin. She now pierced into me with her gaze of predatory silence and I succumbed to her rules. Muttering the true figure in defeat I realized that I no longer had an appreciative audience. Well, I had tried to win back some integrity from this ritual but my game of subterfuge was getting me into further trouble I imagined. 'It's timing and surprise, you fool,' I reproached myself for having lost her favors and my comedic status.

"What day is it, today?" she continued. My mind was nonplussed and I blurted out, Tuesday. Glancing at the calendar on my watch I realized that it was Thursday. I was truly stumbling in this maddening test of my nerves and conventional whimsy. I was stubbing my integrity with every new moment. I felt beaten down and adjusted myself in the chair. But how was I to know what day it was? I was working only part time, three days per week. I no longer had the monotonous register of my days by forty hours of work and the weekend nor was I attending school. And I suddenly longed for it to be tomorrow when I would be comfortably at work. Startled by her next question, I awoke from my reverie.

"Would you tell me when a minute is up?" she asked gravely. Nervously I slid my finger to my pulse guessing that, in this distracting climate, my heart rate to be about eighty beats per minute. 'Now,' I nearly shouted, happy to be done with this silent count. Our time was up! Through the fog of neon light I saw her stand as she began to summarize her diagnosis. I listened with mild amusement, running my fingers under the chair, searching for any evidence of hidden microphones.

Her verdict was in. It was the beginning episodes of a psychosis. "I should fill this prescription," she said very quickly, as if she was running late. I should take one tablet before bed and she would see me in one week. My mind began to stir from the well orchestrated hypnotism of this session. I scrutinized her, locking horns, so to speak. She looked at me coyly now, as if she was reading the very secrets of my soul, disinterring my deepest thoughts, and palming them with some conceit. Meanwhile, I thought to myself, if I am but this mask to her who is truly deceived she has merely transformed and reverted, through her own suspicion, to the subject of her own inquiry!

I worried with some confusion over the convoluted style of this thought and walking out, I muttered impatiently, schizophrenic-midwifery-humbuggery! Why we can even abbreviate it, S.M.H., I rejoiced. The wellspring of a psychosis, eh! Well, I suppose, even I wouldn't forget the further reaches of pioneered space. A moonwalk! Oh, to be sure, I scoffed. Is that why I am bursting with lucidity?!! And I pounced on her diagnosis as an affront to me making sure, all the while, that I kept as quiet and calm as my little Buddha. As I departed I noticed a man sitting at a computer across the hall. I continued to confer with myself, as if with my best friend. How far had 'big brother' come with the advances of technology and how far had they gotten with me?

The air outside never felt quite so magnificent. I smirked with a wry smile, S.M.H. anyone! In this modern world you derive satisfaction from making me do cartwheels before this strange public eye.

Call me a fool, I stammered, but presently I couldn't walk fast enough. My mind was racing and I couldn't account for what had happened to me in that office. With what on earth had they drugged me? I knew that I could never document what had transpired. It was all so frightfully new and I was unaware of all of the particulars. I began to ask what others might do in a similar situation. It seemed as though the entire world had turned from me. Thus I whipped myself good. Calling myself an idiot, a puppet, a clown, and a bag of tricks I scampered to my car, the leaves blowing with grave imminence across the parking lot.

Soon clear reasoning returned to me, thank the powers that be, and I began to plumb the depths of my situation. I felt the strength of yearning survival come to the fore. I was privy to this branch of medicine, its imperfections and weaknesses left ignored. What a scowling performance of intimidation. The maieutic method passed down through the millennia to every self righteous lawman, doctor, and attorney. Merely a form of making others timid with smug exploitative and terrible fury. Answering a question with a question, I sneered. What a ploy for dupes and scholastic nitwits. But my confidence began to wane. Why had nobody taken me seriously? Why did they doubt the undeniable circumstances of my predicament?

Again, I recalled the phenomena of antagonism; the P.I., the telephone message, the attorney, and lastly, the psychiatrist. Perhaps this doctor had been put up to her performance by foul means. Maybe theis prescription was for nothing more than a placebo. Had I, at one time or another, born witness to something I should not have heard nor seen on this earth? The impersonal distance and abstract kindness of all of these players certainly pointed to the jeopardy of my situation. In fact, it seemed to breathe life into every fledgling fear so that with each new acquaintance I became more suspicious. Oh, well, I'll toss these pills into the sewer and drug an alligator, I pledged, with a lead foot upon the gas pedal.

The next morning at work I sat in the dark examination room lit by a small, fluttering neon lamp. My machine was humming with undulating waves of vibration. I began to become aware of a rather piercing noise and quickly picked up the transducer piece. Pressing it to my ear I listened to its encased crystals oscillate like the components of an atom. Dazed by this eerie noise and the electricity from the lamp, I recalled the countless hours that I had spent glaring at this monitor. Looking at these small, charcoal-like etchings of bone and tissue in studious silence could not possibly be good for one for long. I tapped at a medical publication upon my lap sinking now into discouragement. How many hours, days, years had I seen one patient, then another, turning each inside-out with this miracle wand. Yet I came to really know not one of them. Nor did I come to know as a friend any of the employees. It was always the predictable sameness, always thin bitter coffee and the pain of patients suffering our dutifulness. Hadn't one of my patients, just the other day, asked with some astonishment and dismay "is this all you do everyday?" I had laughed it off at first. But now, as many years earlier, I questioned the sense of this endeavor. Was the isolating and pathologically-oriented nature of my work beginning to infect my own life? Could one truly separate his labor from his life as if it was as easily removable as a medical smock? 'Professionalism,' you say. Doesn't anybody see beyond such language? The only appropriate gesture after being swindled by one of these professions is to fatefully sigh and shrug one's shoulders.

With much more distinction, glory, and deference it would be wise to walk this earth a tramp, or better yet, an aborigine on walkabout! My thoughts trailed off, thinking of shaggy silhouettes upon stone and water. Oh, but I should have been a shoemaker, I thought to myself, and avoided this royal family pretext of medicine robbing people of their dignity and their hard earnings. So much for the base nature and heartache of our dilemma.

There was a knock at my partially opened door. I could only make out a gathering of darkness and I leaned to turn on the ceiling light. 'Yes,' I inquired. It was, I could now see, a repair man. He asked if it was convenient for him to take a look at some electrical problem. I told him that my next appointment was not scheduled for one-half hour. He told me that he had to climb up into the overhead space in order to trace the problem. It should only take a few minutes, he assured me. For the first time I took notice of this porthole above my head and, thinking of my apartment, told him that it would be fine with me. I left the room, my mind partially returning to the hierarchy of my troubles, wondering specifically what it was that this repairman had undertaken. I walked briskly to where the coffee pot was located and poured myself a cup. The doctor came in greeting me joyously, not a novice to suffering himself. In fact, he was one of the precious few whom I enjoyed. His company was balanced with good natured humor. I was proud to work with him, and not for him, and I counted my blessings at this time. We talked in quiet confidence to one another with what seemed to be a kind, affable, and mutual respect.

On the return to my examining room I passed a few of the technologists blind toward me and I muttered to myself, 'pinheads.' Vacation time was coming up in only one week and I felt some happy anticipation with this thought. Entering my office I sat to sip at my hot coffee. The repairman had already departed. A few minutes passed. Then, as if I had been drugged, a new mood began to shape itself across my forehead. It was like being no longer alone, as if something or someone had crept silently into me. In disbelief I felt the visitation of these imps invading the privacy of my thoughts and contaminating my authentic state of mind. 'Jesus, they are here,' I groaned, and I looked down at my coffee with some shock. Perhaps these others were much bigger than first imagined, I realized. What if they were affecting those around me as well? I suddenly felt flushed with fear, afraid for my patients and staff alike.

In need of some support from one who could understand the insidious and offensive nature of my situation, I dashed to the telephone book and I attempted to retrieve the number of my attorney. To my horror I couldn't locate his name. I began to think about this 'Paul Ivy,' in my rising excitement. 'Paul Ivy' or poison ivy I assimilated with revelatory ease. Good lord, I gasped, it was a pretext. That was it. I had enough. No telling who was who anymore. Focusing with all my might I thought about this fictitious lawyer caricaturing my having worked for 'intelligence' and I recalled the interruption of the telephone call during my visit. The quick glance he had given me now stood out with great clarity. This game of predator and prey had become insuperable. I couldn't very well operate at work with this great enemy looming about me.

Possibly the repairman, or goodness knows who lay in wait like sullen, villainous shadows. No I could not take this punishment silently conforming to protocol. I would have to leave now! No time for clumsy confrontations nor fumbling excuses to management. I must run for my life! Darting out the back door, I said not a word to anybody. I drove along the country roads, a fugitive, toward the freeway out of town. Easier to take notice of traffic, I reasoned. But then my pager sounded off, scaring the daylights out of me. I reached for it, shut it off, and tossed it onto the passenger floor with one sweeping gesture. It fell upon coffee cups, license plate numbers scrawled page upon page, and landed by my voice-activated tape recorder I had purchased a few earlier. My priority of values came to the fore. 'Forget work, this is survival,' I exclaimed.

After some time the shock of my trials began to fade. Watching the sun flash through the sad and thoughtful avenue of trees, I finally collected myself and I pulled over to the side of the road. Anxious waves of relief mixed with doom passed dreamily before my mind's eye. Rummaging for a solution I realized that I must take flight. No time for elaborate preparations of moving nor any other considerations. I would go directly home, quickly pack, and buy my ticket at the airport. Yes, I concurred, I will leave everything behind me and reconsider this 'thing' more clearly from the safe haven of a foreign shore.I started the engine and drove cautiously down the road, now comfortably withdrawn and alert, one step closer to the truth!

V

~ Across the border ~

A web of fine, white light spun above the deep, graveled dish of the bay. The road that we traveled from the airport unwound in a set of steep switchbacks through parrot-green. On the slopes of this theater, like spectator's seats, the tiers of domestic terraces fingered gently down into the palm of the sea. The blue sky and lustrous waters below seemed like old friends and they were having quite a salutary effect upon me. I could hardly wait to take a long, refreshing swim. The rollicking bus dropped me off at my designated choice, a seaside hotel. I stood in a line waiting to be checked into my room feeling both free and happy. If anyone were to try and tag me now they would have to do so at some expense and from within a foreign country. That ought to impede any of their progress, whatever mischief this was in which I had become unknowingly involved, and inwardly I thumbed my nose at these demons.

The receptionist was very kind and sweet to me and I felt tears forming inside my heart over this familiar setting of joy in travel. Yes, I could feel my senses opening up now like a flower toward the sunny features of all these good tidings, these merry faces and laughing voices. Everyone seemed to blush with excitement and promise. The premonition of love lay softly awaiting us in the quiet shade or shimmered in the sultry air. I couldn't race fast enough to my room to slip into my bathing suit for a splash in the water. While getting dressed, however, I noticed how dark and lonely the room appeared as compared to the abundant life outside. I walked over to the drapes and, opening them, returned to sit upon the bed. 'There, that is better,' I said to myself. 'Or is it?' I questioned. My moods were passing, deckle-edged with affects. It was as though I was sitting before some silent film, in that poor glimmering technology of motion and lighting. I could feel the sky itself opening up, swallowing the air around me. Light wavered bright, then dim, like shutters being opened and closed, or as if the sun was blinking between fleets of sailing cloud. And I trembled, feeling with each separate tide a small death occurring within. I was in the grip of a fever. It was a fever of perception only, and I felt its wet fingertips flutter lightly upon my eyelids. I raced to retrieve my room key and sunglasses, my towel and a book on graphology that I had brought with me. I wanted to analyze any character change in my handwriting.

Henceforth, I was determined to follow the course of any invasion from these forces about me. I must have let out an audible sigh of relief upon slamming the door behind me.

Perhaps I should sleep on the beach tonight rather than flounder in that tomb.

Meanwhile, I wasn't sure what I should do first; take an ocean swim, lay poolside, or grab a bite to eat. I decided to go down to the pool and have a look at the clientele. Maybe I would while away my cares breathing in the tanning oils of some beauty roasting her loins to culinary perfection, I mused dreamily, and not without some hunger pains. By the time I had entered the hotel lobby I had changed my mind. Noticing an hors d'oeuvres bar half hidden from the check-in desk I ordered some food and a glass of pineapple juice. I quickly consumed them feeling all the better for it.I walked toward the pool and then it struck me between the eyes like some mythopoetic vision-women! Two or three dozen of the most ravishing beauties to walk the earth lay in no more than thongs. Great screaming lust! It wasn't as though I was merely taken by their natural beauty. No, this was something altogether different. No longer was I just a man brimming with desire for my body would spasm and convulse with the slightest of provocations.

A foot or toe, let alone the soft tenderness under their arms and legs, or the unexaggerated sweetness of their escutcheons had me shaking from my roots. I didn't dare looking at the fruit of their mouths, their raving headdress, or the cocoa skin that waved before me wit the scent of a hot, musty apple. Otherwise I would shudder with unrelenting paroxysm. What on earth had someone put into my food and drink, anyway? I wondered with amazement. My mouth was slick and the tropical air smelled of ether. So they're here, too, I gasped. Why had I become no more than this rapacity? Why I am beyond Dracula, I recoiled in disbelief, a dragon or a lion copulating in the hot savannah, slaking my thirst with a thousand lionesses. I will leave nothing left. What a test of my good manners, what a struggle with these claws pawing at my instincts. Play it cool, you ape, I counseled to myself. They were all sent here, no doubt, with designs to take you off your guard. The only thing to do is to keep your head down and maintain some semblance of dignity and order. In a little time I reasoned that the people delighting themselves in the wings of this party were giving more of the drug to some, less to others. 'They' were manipulating the mood of the place as if we were all puppets on a string. 'What tremendous power these people had,' I cried out to myself. But my seizures cameand went, and as I caught sight of a delicious brunette, her lipstick smeared like a cup of hot sherbet, I nearly swooned.

Finally I managed to withdraw from her magnetism and, as I left for the beach, I merely shrugged my shoulders.

My body felt lean and full of a fantastic vitality but my nerves were on edge as I contemplated this unapproachable mythos of creation. A woman strolled by. I didn't dare look. But who was I fooling and who were the players in this game of eroticism. 'They' knew me well; how to control my appetites, my cowardly reticence, and how to isolate me from the human crowd. On the way to shore break, over sand blazing like fire, I began to feel the return of an old mood. It was momentary, as though I had left something behind. 'But what?' I queried, and I started to inventory the paraphernalia of mybaggage. Was it nothing in particular, but instead, more of a part of myself missing?

With this thought mingled a nameless sense of suspicion. But I shook it off as I entered the water, exercising in this new geography of freedom.

The water was like heavy velvet, luxuriously rubbing against me. I would dive down to cooler depths, enjoying as I did so, the voluptuous satin of this element.

There I would stay submerged, playing a game of hide and seek from the loud and violent world. All around me, the swirling diadem of white water mirrored in the brushstrokes of a cloud. As I dried myself off I became aware of an ever so faint presence. However, the thrill of the eternal sea gave flight to all apprehensions. Thus, I was left alone, to no longer suffer from these aphrodisiacs.

Laying there, eyes shut, I soothed myself with memories from my travels to the world's waters, thinking of their different shades of blue and green, and the dark ink of the octopus. But at the same time I became aware that things had changed and their distant, long- lost remembrance filled me with melancholy. I couldn't understand it but a couple walking down the shore trained their camera upon me. I looked at them half annoyed, partly amused by their intentions. They seemed to linger there for some time, self-consciously but dutifully, then went on with their business. As quickly as they had appeared, they vanished into the distance.

Things were beginning to heat up once again and I decided to immerse myself in the blue and white curls of the sea. I wandered down to the seamark in the hot, gritty sand. Watching the froth bubble and wink for a moment, I finally advanced into the surf to enter my new world. After idling away the minutes, spouting water like a cherub, I started to awaken from the canopy of the heat.

I waded back toward the shore a little blind from the glare of the sun. The dazzling light bronzed the beach and I could make out a figure walking toward the water. I brushed my hair back from my face feeling the sting of the salt in my eyes.

Before I knew it I was suddenly standing opposite one of the women who had recently arrived. It was good luck that the drugs had worn off some and that my vision was blurred, I thought to myself. Perhaps they were players as well as the couple with the video equipment. She cordially greeted me and I timorously replied. Bubbly and loquacious, she continued on talking about the splendid beauty of this place. I must admit I felt none too sure of myself and I certainly didn't wish for her to get into any mischief by talking with me. I glanced casually around wondering what had happened to the camera crew, then at her form momentarily, my eyes coming to focus. 'Oof !' I breathlessly cried. A wild thatch of dark curls framed the oval of her face giving the impression of wind, though there wasn't the slightest breeze. She possessed the startled eyes and alert ears of a fawn. Her tender throat sang as if offering the world its measure in praises. Yes, she had a voice made of wind chimes and bells, and when she giggled at one of my comments, as she once did, it sounded like the fresh, crisp purling of water over stone. And her lips were, well, other worldly! Heart attack red, the color of an exotic flower that blossomed once every third millennium. Those petals seemed to imbibe their nourishment from the sultry air. Red, redder, reddest I thought to myself, shifting from foot to foot in my nervousness, and suffering this grammatical declension. Had we met before? I wondered. We continued to speak and, I realized, I was falling madly in love. I laughed for the first time in a long while and I bade her a good swim wondering, of course, if she was on this aphrodisiac as well.

By the time I returned to my towel I was cursing myself for my torn state and introversion. I was shaking like a leaf. I could still softly hear her footfall in the printed sand as she strolled away laughing. I began to become consumed by thoughts of saving her in some daring rescue and emerging her lover and hero. Why, I even went so far as to give her a name. 'I will call her, Victoria,' I breathed. Yes, she must be on this love potion as well, though she obviously wasn't as drugged as myself. That's only fitting, I ruminated, for I was the central focus of this battle, and management, whomever they were, knew their protagonist with dead-eye aim. The heat was beginning to annoy me. I could still hear the waves but I continued to lay within the shadowy nocturnes of introspection. However, I walked back to the hotel feeling some happiness and lilt returning to my stride. 'Red, redder, reddest,' I sung. As nobody was near I chanted, "whatever Lola wants, Lola gets," almost sobbing with laughter. Then, very abruptly, I awoke and retorted irritably, "Ol man Faustus, I presume, forcing a laugh and picking up the pace. But as I approached my new residence I found myself balking a little with both anticipation and renewed suspicion. What was the nature of this drama being played out among all of these strangers? Everyone seemed faint from the heat and either wilted among rafts in the pool or, chaise lounges beneath large umbrellas. Perhaps this was due to the sequela of this love potion, making its victim weary with a sort of post-coital fatigue. Meanwhile I, myself, felt a surplus of energy and I decided to satisfy it with a vigorous walk through the town.

I changed into dry clothes and raced briskly up the street as if I held the key to the city, while the echo of the surf still pounded within my ears.

Some of the hotels were painted in white and aqua and had the appearance of the nineteen-fifties when the town was in its heyday as a resort. It reminded me of my youth and of bygone times when things were slower, less technological, less crowded. This pleased me a great deal. As I was in the mood for something cool and delicious, I stopped abruptly at a concession stand. Ordering some fruit-flavored ice I sat in the shade at a patio table to appreciate my refreshment. A few minutes passed and a couple strolled in from the main boulevard. I didn't hear them speak but presumed that they were French having seen the man with a pack of French cigarettes bleues sticking halfway out of his shirt pocket. They collected their order and sat across from me. With some surprise I found myself speaking to them in French.

They invited me to sit with them and I eagerly complied. Suddenly, the happy mood of travel came over me. Meanwhile, while discussing our places of origin to one another, two policeman entered the stand.

The Frenchman must have noticed my eyes wander in their direction for he turned toward them himself. Turning slowly back he uttered, "so and so," the names of two bumbling detectives of television. I laughed out loud at this analogy and the ridiculous nature of television propagated around the world. It felt so good to be with these people by the sea laughing like old times that I forgot all that had happened to me for a moment. "Ils sont a couvert," I responded, at which point he laughed, offering me a cigarette. I exhaled dreamily, watching the smoke slowly drift up into the air. It seemed that they were, coincidentally, staying at the same hotel. My attention now fell upon the expressiveness of the woman. As she argued with her husband about the exact cost of a flight to another city they had visited she paused and puckered, distending her cheeks, then blew out a small trail of air. As though forming the uvular trill of the French 'r' her lips seemed to flutter, searching for a kiss. Suddenly, as if stepping out of a Renoir, the rosy petals of her lips leapt toward me, making me convulse uncontrollably. Fortunately, they were too involved to notice my reaction. It was simply a common expression, native to her land, and I had seen it a thousand times, having visited their country. However, now it attacked me in the same visceral way as the phenomena had at poolside some hours earlier.

Had somebody laced my ice or this cigarette with this heady substance again?

I turned my eyes from her sunlit beauty toward a pushcart and abruptly bade this couple 'good luck' and 'goodbye.'

They both responded simultaneously, "a bientot," and I thought to myself, not if I see you first.

Feeling, once again, invigorated by this erotomania I stepped out onto the hot side-walk. Walking up the stifling boulevard, headed to nowhere, I anticipated new and wild adventures over the horizon. After parading passed vendors and a variety of shops for a few blocks, I noticed the ever present tourist with a camera or sport shirt, closing in upon me. Perhaps these French visitors, who, as I have said, were staying at the very same hotel, might be implicated themselves. Maybe they were a miniscule part of this argus-eyed giant? But were they a part of those watching silently over my welfare or my enemy? Who, after all, was turning the screws?

If somebody had a lengthy dossier on me they would know that I had traveled to France and enjoyed their food, culture, and countryside. Would it not be too far fetched to assume one of these elements was trying to appeal to my tastes by various means?

Was it so outlandish that matters had become of international importance, whatever trouble I was in? And I began to admit the plausibility of this avid research organization now trying to get at me through my likes and dislikes. I knew that I had heard of such set-ups on countless documentaries, outlining a course of infiltration into a subject's life that might even require years of planning and execution.

I sat down upon a salt-eaten bench to further appraise the situation. Yes, I concurred, in view of my recent troubled times this could very well be one of those occasions. Had someone along the way, at one time or another during my travels, slipped something into my luggage? Isn't it true that traveling alone sometimes invites one as a mere dupe or scapegoat for such underhanded dealings? Could it not be possible that this project had been going on even longer than I suspected and was only now generating itself with overt force?

My financial situation had changed rather

abruptly this last year as I had begun to contract myself out for work freelance style. A sudden change often looks suspicious to the I.R.S., the D.E.A., and other such agencies, doesn't it, I queried. My passport would easily reveal that I had visited the Netherlands, the Bahamas, andThailand in the past. Were these not places that offer up contraband to those interested? Had I consequently been placed on somebody's list? If there had been a mistake made on some secret agencies behalf how would I ever possibly correct it? I shook my head, marveling at the speed of these new reflections integrating all loose ends into a tight knot for my final scrutiny.

I returned to my hotel under the puffs of cloud to take a nap from the day's travels and heat. Awakening to a lambent light I crawled out of bed and washed my face.

Scrambling downstairs to join in on the festivities of the evening I noticed a full moon.

Hungry from the day's exercise I

ordered a large meal at the hotel and sat in the patio. Tapping my fingers upon the table I uneasily watched the guests mingle with one another. Soon my dinner arrived. Typically I would not have had any problem finishing it off with my appetite. However, after the first few spoonfuls each bite became a labor and soon I gave up on trying to clean the plate. Tramping down to the beach I passed by lovers, arm in arm, and by an occasional local making tracks homeward from the day's work at one of these tourist facilities.

The moon, as though stamped by an impression of our lands and seas, glowed from high up in the sky. The waves tilted gently like an hourglass into the sea. In contrast, I trudged along, forced to accelerate my pace to this new, internal clock.

The next morning I awoke to find the hoary skies were dimmed with clouds. Of course it was still warm, but a brief rain was imminent. In the bathroom's mirror I consulted my image. My expression seemed wooden and my eyes, sad and vacant. Their pupils looked as tough they were swimming in a drugged flux. It was as if their smile had become mortally wounded.

By the pool I sipped at my coffee and passed the day lounging and swimming. The French couple joined me for a few hours, idling away the day. Later in the afternoon I took a stroll down the lavender shore, then proceeded to walk the main boulevard. A light shower fell and the thirsty ornaments of plant life dangled like cups to catch the falling rain. The great galleons of cloud crowded darkly above the harbor. Welcoming the shift of spirit from this determined, moody storm I decided, quite naturally, to duck into a restaurant for some cover and conversation. As I entered I could hear the laughter of celebration coming from the bar. I went over to join in on the festivities and took a seat. There was a large group of tourists drinking and trading humor. The affects of this merriment was contagious and I felt the menu of my senses deepening. One of the party was a woman who possessed those fascinating dark eyes of desire. I had to make a conscious effort to avoid looking her way. My infatuation from her spell had me on edge but laughter awakened good feelings from my former world. I quietly smiled but I felt self-conscious after some time. One, it would seem, could detect the weight of my troubles. My drink arrived and I sat quietly watching the restaurant's entrance. I reflected upon my life; love, melancholy, and mischief. I was growing older alone. I finished my drink and raced out into the street. A sudden squall struck from the sky. My head was spinning from the gossip in the lounge. The nuptials of my senses were working havoc from the heavens above. I began to race down the street like a child, jumping happily over the puddles from this downpour, tasting the jasmine-sweet rain. The wet and dusty streets were now starred with brilliants. The rain continued to fall like glad tears from the angels of my memories. I was caught ecstatically stilled in time. It was as when one smells a particular fragrance or tastes a special dish, and my senses burst with joy. My regimen remained and the next day, as usual, I proceeded to trim some of the excess of my nerves with a bath in the sea. Each time I entered this deep, blue bowl of the bay my wishes seemed to be momentarily satisfied. Underwater you could feel the earth rumble and its tables shift a hair. Rubbing shoulders with the sea seemed to be my only solace now. Within her arms the luminous capsule of each thing upon shore would melt away, exposing its fertile image. 'Yes,' I would confide, 'I had much to be thankful for in my life.' At the hotel's pool I lay back, regaled by the tales of this French couple and their night out on the town. The mermaids were still swimming by, delighting everyone's eyes, cooling the burning fevers of their rapture. You could hear the blue-marbled sea soughing its hush and the heavy breathing of lust settle. The evening's transparencies were falling to earth like a silk slip. Finally the day was coming to a close. This twilight was my savior when courage was running low. It was the moment when one's life comes true. At this bewitching hour I would tremble with the ensanguined horizon. Neither blinded by the harpoon of day's light nor made lonely by the dark night, it was always the best time to dine and to laugh. The days came and went and the same circumstances and coincidences presented themselves with predictable frequency. In my heart I was sickened at the idea of my return but, nonetheless, considered it best to confront the inevitable. I was learning how to become quite the consummate actor and I applauded my own efforts more than once.

All trades have their tricks. Why shouldn't I be able to adapt to this new world, I reflected. No, I wouldn't have anymore discouragement. I was a player, like it or not. And why not enjoy it even if it is on such a spectacular scale. If only I could sit still and be spared of these brittle nerves. I walked to the poolside bar and placed my order. In the calm of my last swim I slowly, methodically, sized up all of these idlers. Complacently, I sat, taking them one by one, hand in hand, so to speak, placing them in the ledger of memory.

I took a long drink and gazed briefly at one of these rare beauties. I turned toward the bartender for a reprieve from this compelling drug, my eyes wide open. He seemed to notice my reaction and intoned, "very beautiful, no?"

I agreed, with a simpering smile, wondering what it was he had put into my drink and from whom he took orders. I halfway expected all of these actors and actresses to come out and take a last bow before I left for the airport. But no such thing happened. Instead I lounged in the liquid afternoon, a captive, feeling the tremulous affects of this mighty elixir. No doubt, this was a source of amusement to this organization and a reminder, upon my departure, of who was boss.

VI

Week after week merged more anonymously into one another, dragging me head first, more deeply into this nightmare. Retiring into a state between that of prayer and dread, I would sit in a darkened corner wringing my hands devoutly. My thinking at times had become desultory and, as a result, I began to simplify, thereby better accommodating communication. It was an enactment of correspondence that now demanded a more facile and primal approach toward my awaiting public. Consequently, I would invest my efforts more ceremoniously in concert with this new kingdom of survival and attuned to others play-acting. Silent and withdrawn, I would meet each new surprise quite unsurprised. Neither giving my enemies the pleasure of any outward emotion nor allowing the burden of the moment to divest me of my dignity, I walked 'my' walk toward 'their' gallows. Nonetheless, my usual skittish humor was being slowly displaced by a morbidity I had never before known. Periods of great confusion and fear were punctuated by revelations of lucidity. As if, by intuitive leaps and bounds, I was able to perform miraculous discoveries. Ferreting out subtle distinctions and vague associations with magnificent ease, I would paint the composite picture with just the proper choice of hue from the palette of my thoughtful soliloquy, as declarative as bunting.

I would begin enormous projects, only to be abandoned the very next day for new ones. Novels would be frantically drawn and outlined in illegible handwriting. Endless lists of preoccupations and endeavors could be found on scraps of paper littering the apartment. Notes and memoranda; from joining a bird watching society, an archaeological dig, or learning how to dance or play the clarinet, cluttered the marginalia of partially read magazines and newspapers. It was as if it was my last hour and this capsule of time needed to be both expanded and exploited. If death was near, why not enter the world of unrealized goals, I must have thought at the time.

Henceforth, I would not only exhaust all of the content within previously placed borders, but would move the impedimenta of these boundaries to include the entire world. 'I will usurp hopes and dreams never realized by one man alone,' I remembered shouting aloud.

However, all too soon, the monomania of one of these rare outbursts would become suppressed by a dull sadness. I would slowly become captured by the fatigue of labor involved in these enterprises and I would lay in a stupor of melancholy. There I would idle to ponder the noise of some falling object next door, gurgling to myself and muttering incantations, partial thoughts, and wordless prayer. Then, after this pause of inertia, I would finally recover. Scrambling toward my pen I would pummel the paper with jabs of new ideas, new insights, and fantastic pyrotechnical discoveries. After filling every square inch of the paper I would collapse, exhausted once again. The next morning I would awaken to nothing more than indecipherable hieroglyphics scribbled in every direction upon the crabbed paper.

My body began feeling lighter and lighter as the days wore on. A surge of nervous energy accompanied by a rising sexual lust seemed to mark my actions and redefine my thoughts more and more as well. I so often sat perplexed by my new situation while what appeared to be small motes of dust landed upon my face. I would hear a crack as in the expansion and contraction of the walls, or from within the television set itself, or upon the furniture cutting deeply, mercilessly into me. No longer a slight noise, it sounded as loud as the snapping of a fresh carrot. Then my attention would turn toward the humming refrigerator. As though the inanimate was growing wild with a secret life of its own, every noise-making object became a source of both suspicion and disgruntlement. As I could not trace the origins of this 'dust' I began to attribute the intrusion to an external, foreign source. I also associated its presence with the cracking noises about me.

Some external force was patently responsible for this untidy mess of my life. That much was certain!

About this time, if memory serves, while scouring the pots and pans with steel sponge the sharp grinding would eat into my very soul and the voices of my neighbors would rise and whine. I could make out two repetitive expressions.

'Amazing' and 'do you believe this man' somebody would hoarsely whisper. Although it took all the attention that I could possibly derive, these imps were naturally both hidden and quite near. And so it was that with my moods and fear I began to firmly associate the surveillance about me with some hypnotic control over me.

I would place large, black trash bags together upon the white tiled floor and later scrutinize them meticulously for any specks of a foreign substance. Later, barely discernible to the unpracticed eye, there was overwhelming evidence of some foreign intrusion. 'Birds molting through a sieve upstairs, I would say loudly enough for any listening ears to hear. And I would continue, 'you must be myna birds mimicking me with a voyeur's joy!'

Occasionally, I would bang the broom against the ceiling trying to ruffle the feathers of these nesting warblers. Oh, but they were adamant and, strangely enough at times, became my fair feathered friends.

Seemingly, they were interested in my welfare and direction like some hidden muse. At other times their very source of meddling hurled me into a state of chaos.

As a result the furniture and I would engage, at its peculiar bidding, in long and winded discourse. Rather methodically they would lay my soul bare; the vivisection of each plane, every aspect of my thought and experience plundered relentlessly. It was a game of thrust and parry, or perish.

Thankfully, I arose to the occasion with the enthusiasm of necessity. But their deceit had me reeling to their inquiries with clouded exegeses. Yes, responding one way or another to these fretful analysts occasionally left us in a form of curious companionship. As though the flag of truce had been raised we would quite often disengage exhausted yet in good humor. The coexistence of these phenomena and the powdery evidence, or what have you, upon the floor disabused me of any guilt associated with the perpetration of myths about my crisis. Thus the depositions had been delivered, testimony was clear, the verdict was guilty. But of what - struggle, love, loneliness? The properties of my new senses and ideas were beginning to mingle in independent ways. It was as though I was being controlled beyond my will from some great alchemist collaborating within the walls of my fortress. I began to assume the moody attributes of a new form of causality and I became suspicious of all electrical apparatus.

Especially, of computers. I no longer lived with any form of complacency, nor in a world of seasonable certainties.

Instead, I lived on the fringe, inhabited by the shadows of apocryphal revelation and beneath the umbrella of suggestions and coy whispers.

I began performing experiments with this epiphenomenal world trying to squelch its presence. I would cover up my ears, put on headphones with music, or take a dip in the pool. But alas, it was of no avail! For in thus being submerged or blocking out sound, one way or another, the presence of these menacing intangibles never entirely disappeared. With whatever interference I would run against them they would seem to answer back a decibel louder. Since the advent of this tireless din my nerves were, of course by now, quite ravaged. I became, at once, both exhausted and alert in a privileged sense.

The television news appeared more than ever like a silly puppet show. 'You jackals,' I would cry, 'simply more confidence men, the graft of this world all about me!' I couldn't shut it off quickly enough. What was the meaning of the encroachment of these hunters and trespassers everywhere I went? I would, once more, ask myself. As if this estrangement from people and all forms of media was not enough, the walls cracking would toss me into a state of alarm. In this new world order the sacred threshold was something not only to be denied but trampled upon as well. No rights, certainly no privileges, and absolutely no limits that were properly respected. The unbroken trail of whispers, quiet though they sometimes were, assumed a formidable posture and consequently appropriated an inveterate state of vigil. Thus, every voice or faint meandering was a stone not only to be unturned but to deflect back to these meddlers with an ephemeral hurrah!

Turning off the lights and sitting in the hallway of meditative darkness, I would prick up my ears intrigued by the death-like emptiness biting into my patience. Sooner or later something like the scamper of mice could be heard. Occasionally I would hear 'them' speaking irritably to one another and fumbling about. No doubt, in a panic and frustrated at having lost track of me. Then I would burst out into almighty song celebrating my victory at this hide-and-seek with deliberate revenge. Obviously, I was no more than a keepsake toward which these superior numbers had grown ambivalent. On the one hand, they would shower me with the blandishments of a long-absent prodigy. On the other, they would wield their wicked language of stubborn banter only to deracinate or console me as their whim might be.

I began to drink more heavily and to start earlier. Alcohol seemed to be the only way to get free from the assailment of this evil datum. Even though it was only momentary any reprieve from this world of noise was quite welcome. In the beginning this was my panacea and I falsely attributed its favorable result to the chemicals it possessed not being synergistic with those of the great alchemist, the brains of this siege. This nameless agency with whom

I was engaged in mortal combat, well, they knew how to spin me like a top. Though I felt imprisoned by the walls of my apartment, I felt equally frightened of the outside. The world was nothing more than the continual collaboration of traffic, mechanical histrionics, and menacing eyes. This hustle and bustle of cars had grown a thousand fold, multiplied around me like great rings of sound. Any of the dialogue that I would overhear, no matter how simple, was brimming with innuendo pointing to these secret forces at work in my life. Despite the occasional glance of apology, I was never able to forgive these meddling strangers. It began to take longer and longer to mentally prepare myself for any confrontation with these other elements and, accordingly, I would stock up on groceries for a week at a time. When I did leave the apartment I would leave a cookie and a glass of milk behind as when a child leaves something for Santa on Christmas Eve. In this way I would let them all know that I was not only immune to their methods but that they had themselves become my hobbyhorse, my swine to be driven into their pens.

It was the end of spring. I felt as if I was seated at a gaming table, the ceiling was alive with unseen visitants. Upon the sofa with a stack of paper I began to write out my messages.

'Who are you,' I wrote in large, bold letters. 'What do you want, what have I done?' I asked. Furthermore, I wrote down a request, asking them quite simply to give me a sign of some sort. Then I concluded my message telling them that I would be at the corner coffee house awaiting their arrival. I shuffled them in order leaving the first one on top of the coffee table for those above me to see. I could hear a quiet set of voices and, I believe, two pairs of slipshod shoes taking muffled steps upon the attic space. No doubt, they had become troubled with some impatience over my inquiry.

I had a second idea. I would ask them to knock once for yes, twice for no. I wrote on a separate piece of paper 'are you with a government agency?' And I heard one loud bang, like a shoe had been thrown against a wall. Then, all of a sudden, I heard two more taps. So they were still set on puzzling me, I thought. No matter, I breathed, I will continue with my original plan. My travel bag and a few important papers had been, in my anxious condition, quickly and carelessly packed. Somebody at some time had purposely, no doubt, broken one of the hasps of my suitcase.

Undeterred I bundled it closed with some rope. The remains of furniture and clothes, of dishes and miscellany, were left for the ruthless scavengers awaiting my inevitable departure. I grabbed the car keys and my luggage and headed out the door greatly excited, reveling with anticipation.

Pulling up softly to the curb by the coffee house, I turned off the motor. I would sit and wait patiently as I had done so many times before. After some five minutes a man with a cap entered the van parked less than four yards in front of me.

He glanced my way, then down at the

ground, as if weighed down by his mission.

My eyes dropped to his license plate, PPA365, it read. It felt so much like a staged setting anyone, it seemed, could read its final meaning. So that's what undercover is all about, I sighed, and I realized at once what the license plat meant.

'Public Protection Agency, three hundred and sixty-five days a year.' I immediately felt somewhat guilty about endangering this man, risking his life as he was. I drew my eyes quickly from his car and license plate for fear of giving him away.

Looking casually around I noticed a mother sitting close to her baby's carriage near the front entrance of the coffee shop.

The afternoon light sadly trembled upon her resigned face. They undoubtedly knew everything about me, I now reasoned, not without a tear in my eye. For it was flawlessly clear that they meant not only to protect me from these evil forces, but that they were also employing personnel that would provide soothing nourishment to my unsteady self. A woman and a child! What more beautiful setting could they have provided me than this eternal Madonna.

Yes, the world had changed and I had stupidly only made purchase upon a distant tremor! It's character now born out of each and every common expression; apprehensive and solemn, longing and alert, the poker face of a bad hand. I began to feel the sad beauty of everyone around me with a gratitude unknown before.

I started my car, not wanting to further endanger anyone in this dreadful game. I had my resources, I replied to myself of this challenge. Burrowing deep inside for a deadly form of patience, I could feel the air around me plaintively cool.

Pulling out into what seemed to be the ceremonial lull of traffic , I headed in the direction of the freeway. Once I had reached the entrance I could see this traffic stalled as in some great funereal procession led by two highway patrolman in the distance ahead. At a crawl I surveyed with a trembling heart the long, sad queue of cars for miles ahead. A new phase of this deadly siege had come to pass. I now felt the heaviness of spirit that a soldier must feel on the way to battle. Feeling a little overwhelmed by the vastness of my plight, I turned on the radio for some comfort. There a Latin rhythm played and, in the background I witnessed the voice of a good friend reassuring me of my safety. The immeasurable vigilance, caring, and insidiousness of this entire affair dumbfounded me. I looked around at this colossal throng of human traffic in shock, tears rolling down my face. Finally I was realizing the full impact of my troubles and the rampant danger implied by these super implied telecommunications. I switched the channel expecting to find more of these messages but I was soon disappointed as I could only hear the clamor of traffic speeding up toward the horizon. Some of the cars, presumably from the P.P.A., bullied ahead prodding the slower, obdurate traffic to clear the way. Whom were the criminal elements among this herd? I questioned.

Something told me to stay behind the big trucks that occupied the slower lanes and use them as protective shields. This I did beset, as I was, by this scourge of traffic angrily racing through space like stray scattershot. From now on I would not let on to anyone, but I would play this mute game with all the dignity I could possibly bring to bear.

Looking up at the sky the sun appeared as the great, eternal eye. It burned as magically as it had when it appeared in my room in a dream at the age of four. No, I would never forget that dream nor this moment, I pledged to myself, nor the numberless responsibilities that lay ahead.

Suddenly I felt insulated and a delightful sense of well being come over me. It was as if I was protected by heaven above. For me it always resided in the mortal face of a loved one. It was the only heaven worth suffering for or worth imagining. Well, whatever follies I had committed from now on I would do what I was capable of and the rest would be up to fate and the good will of the Public Protection Agency.

Though I felt physically alone, desperately, irrevocably alone, I felt somehow lonely no more. As though, you see, that in the breaching of this holy place, from within this jewel of spirit I was finally forced to break bread and take shelter, to sleep and bathe, to yawn and muse, to reckon or not, with myself, alone and forever, a prisoner without walls.

After a few hours of somber travel I turned off this road to nowhere and fled to a motel. I registered and scurried to my room, locking myself inside. I flung the keys down upon the bed and prepared myself for a hot, soothing shower. While drying I took notice of my distant body in the distorting, steamed mirror. A toilet somewhere flushed and it filled me with infinite terror. The pipes shook and wailed like the entrails of some alien beast.

Exhausted I fell hard upon the bed as if it was the bathroom's frosted looking glass. Shattered, I held onto myself, smothering a script of horror. Beneath me the enameled, dirty sheen of the bedspread felt sticky and alive. A door slammed in the distance like an iron fist. My tongue was tied with desperation and I begged mercifully inward for the refreshing cisterns of dream. The pink walls coiled like intestines about me. The fan was writhing fiercely into my ears. My enemy was crouching dangerously close to mutter and chant inanities. For the first time in my life, the first time, I truly wished that I was somebody else. Meanwhile, the surging water from the plumbing tumbled above me, secret rumors spread, while I lay only half alive, tucked into the uncertain arms of my fate.

I dare not speak much further;
But cruel are the times, when we are traitors. And
do not know ourselves; when we hold rumor from
what we fear, yet know not what we fear,
But float upon a wild and violent sea
Each way and move.

~ Shakespeare ~

In the wee, wincing hours of the morning, dreams lay hidden within dreams like a Chinese puzzle. Their panels slide with a precipitous nudging toward realities unfore-seen.... The moon stares like an owl. The seed has long bourgeoned into wild, spring gardens and succumbed to the heat. Orion watches with his bow, waiting for something to happen. The shadows blow like frantic puppets in the darkling ravines. The beast's breath becomes as still and blue as midnight. All noise and motion becomes crime and....

–R. Chaffer

Part Two

I

I sat up in a cold sweat, wishing that I was a wolf so that I might gnaw my leg from this trap. Though this snare I couldn't see, the hound dogs were everywhere. My mind became consumed in stages and tiers to the suck and swish of the plumbing and the angry buzzing of the air conditioners around me. I marveled at the insidiousness and cunning of the invasion as everyday objects leaked into my brain with such alarming detail and exquisite precision.

Each sound, each nuisance searching, as fingers probing in the dark, the very content of my thoughts. Moreover, this foul and seditious noise possessed a peculiar form of fear and veiled script like the humming of an electric wire between my ears. As imperceptible as the lean petrol of a digested meal, sensation now coiled and recoiled snugly into my inner world. While I had slept the doors had swung open. The hunters were upon me. An even more cruel edge of this curse lay at my doorstep.

Reclining thus in my Jonah's whale, exhausted yet alert, I felt not only the center of everyone's focus, but a reluctant hero, a rare property of the world itself. I began to rock to and fro to this murmuring. The restless walls not only had ears, but peeping eyes as well. This I slowly gathered from snatches of commentary, fragments and words and syllables, that would explode with meaning, so intimate were they with my actions and thoughts, like that of twin siblings.

My experimentation continued without surcease but in the final analysis I was no more able to deduce the nature or exact meaning of this 'other' than in the beginning. So, like a caged animal, I paced back and forth racking my brain for a solution and walking off my discouragement. I began to polish the cutlery, as it were, strengthening the rhetoric of my 'yes' and my 'no,' thinking only of survival and adaptability.

'Let's not forget the star of the show,' I said in a low, reproachful voice, strangely surprised. I felt the adrenalin of battle. My mind was clear, cold, and focused. My body roared with resolve. Wake up, sergeant, I heard myself say supportively. It's a clusterfuck, a time to believe only in yourself.

I took a peek out the motel window scanning the corridor and parking lot for movements of any telling sort. A middle-aged man in a red baseball cap was stowing away his gear. The red, white, and blue everywhere, I silently declared in revelation. Yes, the minutemen. Man, woman, and child fighting public enemy number one on the domestic front. No doubt these caps held a special significance.

My struggling apprenticeship was finally outlived. I was a veteran. Privy through my recurrent observations alone, the manners of this game now became absurdly simple. Though the reasons for the grand scale of this deceit, I admit, were still uncertain. Government agents of all ages, sizes, sex, and race were among my entourage. Their appearances, myriad. Yet one thing united them, a solemn air and alertness to the crime that hovered all around us. United in a common, spiritual bond against the lengthening shadows of our times! Well, bless these poor unfortunates, humbled and frightened, even if they do appear a little stiff and incognizant. Like myself, nothing could approach them unawares. Intuition had now thickened into bold and breathing definition. Civilians, no doubt volunteers, the little darlings. Sent by goodness knows who to parade over my well being - the P.P.A.! I scolded myself some over the length of time it had taken me to put two and two together. But who or what, exactly, comprised this opposing evil, I wondered. The answer will come soon enough, I consoled myself. Patience, my dear friend. Nobody can breach this massive deployment. Nobody!

Excited by the sense of freedom that was now mine, I showered and shaved. No longer a simple target wearing a bull's eye, nor chained to a predictable routine, I could watch with a well- measured vigil toward these crews at work around the clock, friends and foe. My shaving kit and clothes were stuffed into my travel bag. I tucked in my shirt and smoothed back my hair, readying myself for the world outside my door. My eyes brushed across the lamp by the bed. 'Let the games begin,' I taunted to my opponents. And I very stealthily crept over to the lamp peering up from underneath and unscrewed the light bulb. From now on I would have to practice every conceivable precaution, exploit every resource. I looked around at the inside of the lampshade and then curiously pondered the filaments within the bulb itself. I wasn't sure of what I was looking for but I knew that these were often places used to plant the nasty little bugs of surveillance. I finally screwed it back in its place with the utmost silence, not altogether comfortable with its appearance. Grabbing my bag and hoisting it over my shoulder, I exited the door like a soldier on furlough.

No sooner had I shut the door behind me when I heard a cough coming from the parking lot. An older man wearing a blue golf cap stood tinkering with a reserve water bottle, fastening it to the tail end of his old camper. Of course, I quickly caught on, 'they' would have to employ every type of person and every form of mobility not knowing where I would go next. As he opened the truck door I came near. I could make out a small national flag hanging from his rear view mirror. I felt, once again, a debt and complicity now with these volunteers. Low ranking, perhaps, with the manners of a goat, but as brave as they were steadfast. I was surprised that they weren't all donned in olive-drab. Though hadn't some of them been just so dressed along the steep and dangerous paths I had walked these last few months.

'Good morning, sir,' I broached impersonally, not wanting to betray the sacred trusts of confidentiality. However, he responded begrudgingly. I immediately realized that I had made my first blunder of the day. Serious business, I thought, filing my error away in memory for future prudence.

Time stood still. Even though it was a sunny day the harsh light hung like a fog.

The birds no longer seemed to sing, but cried instead. Yes, it was a sad day and everyone knew it. Look, I thought to myself, they all walk with their heads bowed or look at nothing straight ahead.

Why, they could have come from any age and nothing, I suppose, would be any different. Just think, if I could only make them laugh. Oh, but I can no longer laugh myself and, if I could, wouldn't I be plunged further into this horrible dream?

Wouldn't I be placing these good people in deeper jeopardy, succeeding only in exacerbating our pain, our distance, our loneliness? Sleep on, dream on, by each far-fetching reach and every means! I mused. Yes, far better to stroke their worried heads with my silent prayers. This strange ambience, this unearthly noise and heavy light, has us all under the weather today.

I nervously sunk into the seat of my car and backed out watching for any changes through the rear view mirror, no matter how subtle. A mother and her child stood loading a station wagon with their belongings. Well, 'they' certainly knew my soft spots, I thought. And I fondly recalled the image of the fair Madonna and her child of yesterday when I had chanced upon introductions to the P.P.A. Such timeless beauty and divine naturalness! Such stamina and wonder; my brothers, my sisters, my silent heroes! The incunabulum to this 'new life,' the throes of which were steadily advancing; if courage was not to entirely desert me, perhaps by an eyelash, I might persevere. Bless your thoughtfulness, I sighed. The child coughed, as had the man in the blue cap, and I began to wonder if this was not some clandestine greeting allowing a brief moment of comraderie between the operatives and myself. The cunning of this gesture clarified my predicament. I felt instantly humbled and adored and scratched at my head knowing they would understand this gesture as my nod of approval and unfailing allegiance to them. Evidently somebody was deeply indebted to me. Was this group an extension of the D.E.A.? Perhaps within their vow to anonymity they had been watching over me since day one, making good for their blunder, no matter what the price. I was simply too naïve to accept such a reality. If only I could make some sort of direct contact and convince them of the adaptability I had at my disposal. Why, with no immediate family and a flexible attitude could I not bring to bear the possibility of disguise and relocation?

However, it was obviously too late for such considerations and I reproached myself for thinking in the past tense. First things first, I ordered to myself, trying to fence in the erratic speed with which my mind was now racing toward uncertain fears and confusion. The answers will come. Patience is everything, I reminded myself, wishing all the while for some remedy. Time for less speculative thinking and more practical planning. I pulled into a convenience store to purchase some milk, coffee, and fruit. The parking lot was filled with anxious, prowling hordes awaiting my arrival. Each seemed to constellate about me in a state of limbo, their eyes painfully averted as if I was a dangerous sorcerer capable of inflicting the abominable curse. While paying for my goods I quickly winked at the store's surveillance camera. Then I returned to my car filching a map from the glove box. I examined the highways and topography as if they were my battle plans.

Raising my eyes from time to time, I sought to witness any observable forms of collusion among my suspicious guests. As I gulped at my coffee my mind seemed to grow more nimble and wary. The lens of my eyes seemed to continually adjust and readjust to accommodate my vision among the mists of tremulous sunshine. I began to feel weak at the knees. Indeed, if I did not act soon I felt that I would be lost altogether. I needed to find a temporary solution. Not necessarily for escape, which seemed impossible, but merely a less expensive hideout where I might swim and dine. Some place to lay low for a while. Some place where I could buy some time. Though I wasn't the least interested in gambling and generally loathed casino towns, I now saw myself drifting toward such resorts for the promise of their 'package deals,' their bargain buffets, and modest lodgings. My lungs seemed to expand and my body relax somewhat as I drove through the open territory of the desert. Cacti, sagebrush, and the occasional tin shed dotted the melting landscape. The traffic, in contradistinction, seemed to pick up its pace, tearing through space at lightening speed, shearing off the rubber from their tires, and squawking like prehistoric beasts.

No doubt this two-headed mob was trying to keep well ahead of me in preparation for my visit. At certain wonderful moments everything became still and quiet allowing my nerves to sigh and to rest. Then it seemed this desert lay like my own senses, raw and exposed to the bright, unrelenting illumination of the sun. As I drove on a barren landscape of ocher waved in the shimmering heat entrancing me, seducing me away from vigilance. However, this vague drowsiness from which I suffered was finally disturbed by one of the glossy casino advertisements and I was able to return to the unfortunate call of these times. Like a mirage, more and more of these displays appeared, announcing the flamboyant oasis of the city. I began to plan my stealthy assault by doubling back, thus confusing them and taking them all by surprise. Graphic posters of celebrity engagements and the promise of being a big winner lit up the road. Dancing girls with garters of cool mint against toffee thighs and hot, pink g-strings with tassels kicked their heels in Saturnalia, welcoming your attendance to another gala event. I skirted past the boulevards sprawling with the minarets of a new Western religion. Shining like mica and costume jewelry, frantic with electrical showers of fireworks, the city seemed to lay under siege itself. Its captors presumably barbarians and doting historians of conquest. It's treasures adorned every street in Technicolor, sparkling like fool's gold. It was an oasis developed by pirates stirring their booty among old, tired lounge acts. Entering from the poorer side of town things began to droop and crouch into shorter buildings forming a less spectacular skyline. You could almost smell the alcohol and nicotine melting like butter upon the gaudy red wallpaper and gummy carpets of these older saloons. Businesses worn thin by attrition or locale, falling into desolate, ill repute from the modern wayside, and knocked into a stupor in the infernal heat of summer, lay like guttered relics. Desperate pawnshops and liquor stores and other assorted businesses stood covered with the latticework of iron gates closed to the end of time.I'll be good for nothing but a vulture's meal, too, if I don't dip myself into a cold pool soon, I thought. And as I began entering the corpus of the city I spotted what I presumed to be a moderately priced hotel. I could always pick up and leave at a moment's notice, I reasoned, should I discover it not to be to my liking. I pulled in, the flames of sunlight licking the hood of my car like a serpent, ready for an awakening splash in the pool. I stood at the check-in desk wondering how they would accept me here being so well surrounded as I was with new, expectant personnel. The one-arm bandits, buzzers, sirens, and flashing lights made me as heartsick as if I was at the circus; where the once-proud and lean instinct of animal now rolled and stood to the crack of man's whip. Preoccupied with this giantinker toy factory and the mock biddings to god's favor in this sad emptiness made me wince with the great pain of our curious separation. No, I never was very fond of gambling and after having waited a few minutes in this clatter-trap I wondered if I hadn't made a mistake in coming. Being the focus in this carnival of light and sound made me feel a bit startled and muzzy, like an epileptic on the threshold of a seizure, and I couldn't wait to dash out of sight.I asked the attending clerk for a room for one. With a brittle face she complied, sliding the registration card forward. I nearly told her that it wasn't my fault that I had brought trouble upon them, adding, a man has to go somewhere. However, I declined, not wanting to further complicate matters and to avoid, I suppose, another instance of theatrical bewilderment. Changing into my bathing suit I quickly flew downstairs to the pool. Alternately lounging and swimming I desperately tried to taper off some of the abundant nervous vigor I felt in my limbs.

Poolside remained fairly empty with an occasional straggler or the appearance of the maintenance man now and then. For this I was thankful. At least they had very wisely arranged for some place of refuge for me. I took full advantage of this spending the rest of the afternoon whiling away my cares, humming with idle thoughts, and some willowy memories of my former life. The heat had taken its toll, even though I had spent most of my time in the shade of an umbrella. I decided to take a nap, resting up for a night out on the town.

However, by the time I had taken a shower and was sitting upon the bed, possessed by the drama that lay ahead, I felt the need for a long walk. Outside the golden pollen of the desert pleased my every sense. In the singed distance hung the umber sky. Dusk stretched and shook out languidly before me like a shade and, in contrast to the light of day, was as cool as fresh linen. This lustrous lotion anointed me to the very marrow of my bones. Even the activity of people and traffic waned dramatically. I walked swiftly block after block, then crossed the street to do the same. Occasionally, from ennui I imagine I would wave at a passing car or nod to one of my aimless, faceless coterie. But after a few rounds of this exercise I began to tire of the resurgent presence of my watchdogs and I entered a casino.

Once inside it was as though I had been rudely awakened in the middle of the night by a loud, tumultuous party. A mixed clamor of voices, glasses ringing, coins dropping, and announcements filled the air. But I suddenly paused, noticing something of a distant force being drummed in. Immense vibrations strummed from the very center of the world seemed to fall like a tenuous net upon all other noises. Like the wailing rain-down through a millennia, ten thousand voices rang out in a storm of echoes. Orchestrated into something like some ancient tragedian chorus it crooned, "we love you, we love you," again and again they chimed bringing a tear to my eyes. I started to marvel at this crafty form of communication, realizing that I was the privileged guest of this magnificent reception. After all, it had to be of some special frequency with which I had been favored or accursed depending upon how you looked at it. Like a halo crowning the glory of having traversed an eternity of confusion and solitude the touching splendor of this new and ingenious disclosure of love chastened me. Enamored, I silently accepted these gentle vows through the auspices of this Giant Global Other, the government, I supposed. But then a chorus of other voices arose into an execratory pitch, "we're going to kill you and anyone who gets in the way," they dictated in mortal sentence. My heart trembled, my knees shook, and I began, once again, to take stock of my rather coarse situation. Shortly, my reason returned. So that was it, I reflected with some aftershock. Both parties were conveying their message to me. Both elements aware, no doubt, of the others communications. It suddenly dawned on me; the attorney was trying to tell me something. No wonder why this colossal secrecy, I thought to myself, and I felt that my sense of self was growing to meet this David and Goliath challenge. Who, I asked myself, was the party from which I could first detect the utterances 'amazing' and 'do you believe him.' What a horrific terror and intrusion, I confessed, and I began to wonder if they could hear my thoughts as well as communicate. However, I left it at that, feeling the need for a drink after my introduction to this disturbing new dimension of the chase. I began to scold myself with deep regret over my diminutive knowledge of science and its vast and impassioned parameters when a woman slunk down upon the stool beside me. I pretended not to notice her and feigned interest in the electronic games flashing at my elbows. In part, for her protection. What possible knowledge would one have to possess in order to extricate himself from this rabid fury of cyberspace and clones dogging my every move? I finally questioned. Meanwhile, my pupils were blinded by the goggling light of this idiot's game.

"Having any luck," she inquired, as though from the backstage of this play. Of course, being no fool at this point, and quite respectful of the power of both parties I answered equivocally 'yes, some.' Though I hadn't gambled since I had arrived, (and, of course, they knew this), my intent was to send a note of some complaint regarding the communications presented thus far to me.

She placed her drink order, then reached down for her purse, her tender breasts bursting for air. My body flinched but I was able to discipline this new reflex somewhat by turning from its source. "See the man over there," she inquired with pouting lips and a pointed finger. "Yes," I concurred, reflexively licking my lips. "At the place where I work as a bartender," she continued, fixing her eyes upon him, "he threatened my life." "Is that right," I responded with some indignation in my voice, reminded of both my phone message from long ago and the daring threat of the night's second chorus. "Well, he won't try anything," I continued, trying to quell her discomfort. "I know," she said "my boyfriend is over there and he's really big." It was quite clear to me that this 'big boyfriend' whom I never set eyes on was simply the incarnation of government force and the man down the way rwepresented its opponent, my opponent. I quickly studied the face of the man unable to imagine any real violence there but, nevertheless, conceded to take it as the warning it was originally intended to be. Somehow her remarks served to return to things their of their human proportion, particularly in contrast to this earlier climate of heaven and hell's shimmering gong. Accordingly I was thankful for this important coutesy. I wished her good luck and I rushed off to mix into the gambling throng, good and evil all around me. I arrived back at the hotel feeling, despite the liquor, that I had just woken up. The actors next door were still at it. The whimpers and suffocating cries, the commotion of furniture rattling, was still being manufactured at thoughtful lulls and peaks.

Stepping out upon the patio I wondered whose eyes were following me from the ceiling, the neighbors, the parking lot, or perhaps, with binoculars from some distance. Sure enough, though it was quite late people strolled about everywhere as if it was an afternoon at the park. Everyone incognito, so to speak. At this point, I reflected, it might be wise to scout around on my own, identifying some of the vital checkpoints. I pocketed my room key, muttering 'balls on a duck' to these impostors next door, and I walked over to the fire escape. No sooner had I opened the door when I heard the clanging echo from a door below. Just like clock work, I thought.

Something insinuated that it was more security and I quickly returned to my room in defeat. There I realized that the momentum had, of course, neither subsided nor abated in this journey. No, I would never be able to escape from either this menagerie of do-gooders nor the hunters, I concluded, and downcast I turned on the television. Keeping the sound down, on alert, I slumped down into the easy chair watching the flickering light upon the walls. The frame rate seemed altered and I began to grow wary of someone influencing me by subliminal means.I awoke early in the morning to the bed banging next door.

What meaning, I wondered, lay in this metronome of copulation? Was it merely a pretext from my protectors or the usage of drugs upon my unsuspecting nemesis? Perhaps they will tear themselves limb from limb and drink one another's blood like bats. On the way to the bathroom I couldn't help but speak out. 'Blood, like wine, with a velvet nose, as sweet as Circe's essence. Don't damage the fangs, Count. Feet like spurs, Countess?' And I laughed at this sly game, recalling the affects of this aphrodisiac upon me, south of the border. While showering I tried to recount part of a poem I once read.

"O precious pudendum of seeming, We come from the Gullible Isles, Where the cannibal complexes frolic And the Mona Lisa smiles." *(Lawrence Durrell)*

Satisfied with my appraisal, for the time being, I trotted downstairs for breakfast curious as to what this lording 'other' had arranged for me in the way of a meal. However, breakfast took place uneventfully and I suffered no secondary side affects. Perhaps this was proof that the P.P.A. was pleased with my ability to cope from within this nodus vivendi? When in doubt walk, I heard myself say. Follow the sure wisdom of the body, not the anarchy of the mind, I counseled. I dug into a jaunty glide down the boulevard, through the fretwork of the streets for some two hours.

Unable to get free of people altogether I began, once again, to despair of my situation. Moods were passing before me like the skies of an Indian summer. The time was soon approaching when I would no longer be able to tolerate this Roman holiday, I realized with some surrender. I began to feel the immense pain of my separation and my suffering began to get the upper hand.To catch my breath from the momentum of the day, I sat in one of the rare geometric designs for some reflection. Around me the vulgarity of architecture mimicking ancient ancestry arose. In the gilt-edged shade, beneath the golden manes of a few palms; in the midst of town, silence collaborated. It felt like Easter. In the thin morning air amethyst volumes of sunlight struck their objects like a peculiar and delicate rain of resurrection. Suddenly, stepping out of this deaf and dumb dream, a woman broke into tears. I was visibly faced with man's worst fear and sorrow - a crying woman. I could feel myself breaking up inside, the ice floes of my vast defense system melting within the warmth of her tears. Her lucid moment.True to her womanhood she had given back life to this otherwise profane and tedious struggle. At least someone finally had the human nature to cut through this gilding. But I couldn't very well console her, thus drawing more attention toward her. Her loyalties and pathos had already been played out!I could almost smell her breath of ginger snaps and violets. Around me a few gimlet-eyed others joined cowardly in her commiseration. Finally, I raced up the street trying to distance myself for her wellbeing. I could not imagine becoming culpable for the crime of having her sentenced to a similar fate. So helplessly I beat at the syllabi of foul language, inviting the wrath of the powers that be or the devil to strike me down once and forever.Though I felt immeasurable cowardice in my retreat there was no other recourse, none, and this I am sure she realized. I entered through a casino door as if it was a magnifying glass into a massive hall of gimcrack décor and the solemn ring of money. I drank down an iced tea praying for the woman's deliverance and recuperating from the blows of her weeping. However, thinking of the night to come and of my difficulty sleeping, I returned to my car at the hotel. I then drove to a pharmacy. My attention, originally, was to pick up an over-the-counter sleeping pill but realizing they would probably be nothing more than placebos, I abandoned the notion. Perhaps, I quipped, I should purchase some jimson weed for the bridal suite next door. Why, with its anti-spasmodic properties it might take the edge off of their bedroom antics, I continued, suddenly feeling very impish. No, I wasn't used up yet, I rallied toward my cause, laughing to myself about my new plan. I bought an ace bandage and proceeded to drive to the location of a store that I had once visited on one of my walkabouts. I knew from listless browsing that they would have a trick or two for my new prankish self.I entered the store and discovered that for which I was searching; a pair of glasses without lenses and, a huge proboscis. I made my way anxiously to the car. There I wrapped my forehead with the bandage, then I donned my new set of spectacles. 'Great spectacle of spectacles,' I punned, looking into the mirror. They'll call me the chameleon and the widows will all weep at my funeral, I laughed, glorified in my new jester's apparel. Just me against the world, eh? Well, I'll show you all a thing or two about the strength of this man and his best friend, humor, I silently countered, beaming all the while at my rejuvenated self. I wasn't through yet! I found in the phone book a costume shop on a street familiar to me. It was, in fact, underlined. Positive proof of these insightful forces at work that had laid their planning well in advance. My lord, I gasped, the enormity of this deceit, the elaborate preparations, and the paper cuts of their logic lay everywhere. I hadn't much difficulty finding it and I entered with an expression of mock seriousness. Confronting the salesperson I very matter-of-factly inquired if she had any ideas for a costume. By now I was beginning to tire of the endless affectation of this play and I didn't much give a hoot about exposing the P.P.A. She giggled and said, "I don't know, what had you in mind?" Such nonchalance, I thought, and I congratulated her inwardly for such a fine performance. My eyes shut, a knowing smile upon my face, I began to reply when a gentleman from outside queried if I had any jumper cables. I, quite naturally, took this to be an omen of some sort. Perhaps they were trying to dissuade me from giving myself, or better yet, their plan away. The plan, that is, of disguise and relocation.

Being always the good Samaritan, I proceeded to help him start his car in a world now lit up with new promise. He asked me about my appearance, my glasses and nose, though of course he already knew who and what I was in this, this audio-colossus! I innocently told him that I was in a play. Then I prodded him gently, you know, by muttering "the play's the thing, wherein I'll catch the conscience of the king" *(Shakespeare).* He looked at me with a smile of complicity and the enormous amusement of a good-natured audience. Then he placed his hand upon my shoulder like an old friend. I was suddenly reminded of the comfort and love of my family and friends. Visiting with them was the only and last time that my fears had subsided since this flying chase began. Finally, I had stumbled upon the old family that man should be, a man with warmth and humor, like my old self, and I was utterly pleased. But the solemn reality of my miserable affairs involving the welfare of others returned, and I began to appeal to my emerging consciousness. Had I said too much? I suddenly felt ashamed, as if I had betrayed these well-doers with my juvenile antics. His conversation was friendly and very much to the point, and his questions appeared after thoughtful refrains. All in all, I enjoyed the gravity of his remarks. He, no doubt, held some high ranking post in this game. He asked me about some component next to my battery. I was never too knowledgeable about mechanics and his question began to arouse my suspicions. Which party, after all, did he represent? Did he represent 'good' or 'bad,' hoping only to discover the subtle methods by which the P.P.A. was communicating with such efficacy? And what about the eerie cracking of the dash filling me with drug-infected mood? Well, I was getting away, it was time to go. My once merry mood had again been replaced with lingering suspicion. I would no longer be an open diary to the questionable ethics of this stranger. I looked at my watch giving him an indication of some impatience and proceeded to make short work of his problem. His car finally started and I curtly waved him goodbye. Meanwhile, I sat uneasily still, hopes dashed, puzzling over this strange apparatus pointed out to me. Was there no end to these rude manipulations? Why had I been spared to speak in metaphor? What clarity was there in the antics of the private investigator, the police, the attorney, or the tongue-tied psychiatrist? I had pleaded my case the best I knew how. Where did that get me? But hadn't I learned my lesson long ago about the dark chambers of the heart slipping into every intellectual system and discipline, every social position. As a child don't we all bear witness to the sophistication of the lie, sense the deceit practiced in the adult world. What could possibly be the reason for this cold cloak-

and-dagger? Nothing but innuendo and fear, punctuated by silence and danger in every exchange. Who could have dreamt of something so terribly wrong from which there was no escape? It's like a damned plague, I sighed. Surely this final defeat of conversation is a telltale sign of the pervasiveness of evil, a pestilence of doom for us all. That night at the hotel I tossed and turned unable to sleep from such wild imaginings. And then from the fan there came a voice, a whisper, embedded in its noise. I recognized it as one and the same with the woman who had sat next to me at the casino only a few nights before. She softly told me to lie still, that 'they' were giving me my medicine. I immediately understood that nobody could tolerate this estrangement and I succumbed to her words. Obediently I lay back, feeling a tingle as faint as a hair across my face. My forehead felt cool, mentholated, as I lay there benumbed from the affects of this invisible powder.

So I was right, I thought. They had been drugging me from time to time and its occurrence was increasing with each new day. I suddenly felt the tactile sensation of fingers meditatively probing my body through the mattress. I was frightened at first but something told me not to get up or give anything away. Furthermore, something seemed to insinuate that this was as close as anyone could get to me and that I needed human touch in my isolation. Tears ran down my cheeks as I stifled my amazement at the cold, broad depths of my dilemma, everywhere, everyday suffering this hash of confusion. I felt infinite thanks to these drugs and I offered up a silent prayer. Then I turned on my side and fell fast asleep, a prisoner of war in my own country. Feeling aloof from these party gatherings I brought a small, dog-eared book of poems to the casino bar hoping to focus on something other than my precarious predicament. This also gave to me some solace, as though I was hearing the thoughtful words of a good friend. Perhaps it would provide a cover from any off-handed confrontations as well. I ordered coffee and opened my book. I was no more than a few lines into a poem when a young, tattered woman sat next to me. Holding onto her glass of whisky as if it was a canteen in the middle of the desert, she finally jabbed at me, "what are you reading?" "A book of poems," I answered softly, sensing the abrasiveness in her voice. However, underneath my breath, I began to curse myself as my planned refuge had presently become a calling card. She asked me if she could see my book and I handed it over to her obligingly, but with some chagrin. She examined a couple of lines with obvious haste, disappointment, and misunderstanding, it seemed, saying that she had written some poetry herself. "Really," I responded without enthusiasm unable to pursue this path of dialogue. I drank down my coffee now in gulps wishing myself away from her. I stepped down off the stool bidding her good luck. She muttered, "go ahead, god damn it, leave." I asked her why she had said that, quite unsurprised, and how had I offended her. My ulterior motive was, perhaps, far too patent; to befriend her momentarily without the slightest reproach, and thus to gain with her confidence the confession of her role, and by implication, the exact nature of my dilemma. She simply replied that maybe she wanted me to stay. I assured her that it was nothing personal and that I had an appointment. We left it at that. I walked away feeling sorry for her having recognized her loneliness. Yet I was truthfully unable to communicate anymore in these troubled times. Anyway, no time for lament, I told myself, she was intoxicated and one breath away from exploding.Was she a decoy of evil or a staunch member of the P.P.A.? Had she merely tested the waters with me and was reaching toward danger far beyond the call of duty? No telling really, I counseled myself, and I trotted off once again.

It was beginning to warm considerably and as I was tired of this suffocating heat and the sad drone of the casinos, I mused about visiting the mountains as a more consoling friend. Almost before I knew what I was doing I had packed and readied myself for this escape to cooler climes. Besides wasn't this form of spontaneity what the P.P.A. probably expected. What with their superior numbers weren't they better adapted to such change as opposed to this netherworld. I suddenly noticed all of the people around me leaving the premises, or so it seemed. Oh, well, what's to be done about it, I questioned. Nothing left but to search for new beginnings!

II

Crossing the desert valley, the air rangout like a cymbal, palpable with the heat fit for apoplexy. I noticed a hitchhiker in the distance. I couldn't very well pass by leaving this poor man to melt. Anyway, he was, no doubt, from one of these two forces and, with any luck, I might even be able to glean some pertinent facts. He scrambled in obviously pleased with the coolness of the car. Demurely he told me his destination with his head down, beaten by this furnace.

I was immediately struck by some similarity to myself though I couldn't put my finger on it.

After indulging in some small talk and an encouraging respite of silence, I began to feel the bristling energy inside me subside.

Stop looking out for yourself, I thought.

Can't you see any longer what is directly in front of you. Nothing less than a brave foot soldier, an expendable, risking life and limb to give you company in your distress. And my exterior began to pause from this wearied self-preoccupation and self pity, though not altogether. Yes, my curiosity got the upper hand. Hadn't he mentioned the approaching solar eclipse? Apparently as reasoning to support his eventual destination, the ocean. Accordingly, I began to pursue a line of questioning.

What, I asked, was the date of the solar eclipse? He filched through his dirty pockets finally withdrawing a sheet of crumpled paper. From my angle I was able to see that it was a calendar month crudely drawn with dates and some form of agenda. He searched for a moment and then recited the day folding this document back into his pocket. Was this my message, I wondered, my rendezvous with destiny, my point of departure from this amorphous world? Then and there I made a mental note of the date and of my new assignation with fate.

Up into the cooler reaches of the mountain pass I became more lucid, realizing only now that my passenger was a messenger of the Public Protection Agency.

Yes, it was imperative that I attend this preternatural event in time. Come what may, I would be there by the ocean on that date hoping his valorous life was not spent in vain. We arrived at an intersection of highway that split our paths and parted company. As he left I offered him some money, greatly appreciative for his communications. He politely refused saying merely that he would be alright. Down the road I pulled over weeping copiously for this man of little means, whomever he represented, the nameless hero. All that I could see through my tears was the faded semblance of a life scribbled on that paper.

Didn't he deserve more than this? Why hadn't he accepted my meager offer? Ah, pride, I answered to myself. That's my good friend, I sighed, nobility of soul in today's crass marketplace. That is something of which we could all use a lot more of these days. Looking over my shoulder I could make out the valley below laying like a dream. The heat rose as from a smoking mirror. The sand appeared to be the smudge of a great fingerprint in hot ash, stones reduced to friable shell through geological time. I could almost feel the bones of my ancestors and the ghosts oftheir hardships. The quiddity of cruel survival lay staring and, aghast, I understood the desperate origin of sacred rituals. I turned on the radio to drowned out the uproar of this silence. It sounded like a cheap cuckoo clock, a rooster crowing with a broken neck. My ears had been pricked offensively by this treble rattle and, in its aftermath, I felt a sensation as if the seat was being heated from beneath me. About twenty minutes had passed when I began to awaken from this lazy drive through the torpid desert. My mind started up in a frenzy with no object at all. My voice box began to vibrate and it became more difficult to swallow. The driver's seat seemed to crackle like a wildfire. I could sense an evil medium of heat reach into me radiating alarm. I placed my hand upon the passenger's seat after touching my own, seeking some comparison. The contrast was striking and my mind was on fire! I began to spit as though by natural reflex to something unnatural happening within. The content of my writhing brain was being rifled with great neglect to my health. Instinctively, I fingered the framework beneath my seat searching for any type of gadgetry that might have been installed by one of these superpowers. The speed of my mind seemed to increase exponentially. Sgfhkla, I roared! Fuming and babbling on and on I clutched at my steering wheel, becoming dizzy from experiencing these small deaths. I could feel legions of tiny cells bursting into infarcts and, stunned with fear, I chattered away nervously. I was being overtaken by this foreign element and I accelerated my car to help vent my rage. Finally, after an eternity, I pulled my car to the side of the road. Unable to take any more I jumped out of this electric chair and scurried over to the woods. My hands pressed to my temples, I begged for mercy from this evil subjection. Oh, Jesus, talk yourself down, talk yourself down, I repeated. It's the only way, I reasoned in my horror. Hum alullaby, anything it takes, I proposed. Walk it off, nothing can hurt you. Simplify all things in this, your hour of darkness. There, that's not so bad is it, I counseled. Thank creation amidst all of this struggle. And I began to come back to my senses after listening to this maternal muse. As if I had fallen a great distance, I stood trembling by the trees. All around me I was suddenly surrounded by a setting as of some great, staged play. The characters of my life came to sit within rekindled memory giving warmth to this darkness and the unknown. Every gesture of reminiscence so noble and inspiriting I could feel a sea of tears rush from my heart, my chest heave to the rhythms of common love. But my life, as I had known it, was at its end. The sun was red and I thought to myself 'red, redder, reddest.' remembering this grammatical declension from my final flirtation with 'Victoria' by the sea. Yes, my humor and sadness was returning as abruptly as it had disappeared. An hour or so later I entered a small town under the ragged shade of immortal desert trees. Like everything else this place, too, had changed. With a head full of worry I witnessed the wan, foreboding light. It wrapped this pillaged town with an uncanny, muffled glow, and in the dour appearance of the empty avenues my heart sank. Yet hadn't I just some few years ago luxuriated in the cool arms of its beauty? Hadn't I laughed with a friend and dipped into ponds as cold as snow? However, the air that once invigorated now appeared fatigued and sat like a thin cloud upon this little village. I am telling you, enough couldn't be said about it! I became consumed by this sleepy light looming about as if its transparencies had been filtered through gauze. Nature retained its genial indifference but suffered this lackluster appearance. The strain of this pursuit had finally chased away any chance of replenishing golden memory.

I took a cabin to avoid sharing walls. I was becoming a recluse as a last resort. If I was to be sacrificed so mercilessly I would choose nature as my graveyard. It was mylast freedom of choice to be exercised and I am sure that, this, 'they' understood. Yes, I will ride this thing alone like death. Aren't we all left alone in the end?

A week had passed before cabin fever

took its raving toll. I was tired of muttering to these faint communications whispering frantically and hiding in fear. Occasionally, I would hear a muffled gunshot as though one of these trespassers had been spotted and cut down by the keen sniper sights of the Public Protection Agency. At one time I could make out the rapid fire of a gunfight as if a munitions yard had been sabotaged. In the rising crescendo of firearms I could feel the intensity of this battle raging. Life and death furiously struggled with one another! Without a weapon myself I was no more than defenseless prey. I would sit crouched by the sink like a small child cringing with fear. My dependency upon these guardians now grew with redoubled trust. Like comrades at arms my undying loyalty deepened. Once the transmissions from my enemy filled the air bragging of their final victory. Convinced and sickened I trembled in a cold sweat. Then I would exploit my patience for a reprieve from these horrors by becoming as still and uncaring as the ticking clock. With time the artifice of their boasting would become confirmed. Soon the mists of silence that precede combat would reappear. Other times I would wonder if this were nothing more than a hoax altogether. At intervals I would fling the door open and march out more than willing to face death. But here I was faced by nothing more than the inkblots of midnight and a faint rustling of the trees. Always confounded by their cowardly hiding I would finally become incensed at their assaults upon me. But not wanting to reveal the fear that is anger I would beat them back with only a sly remark. Such instances almost exclusively occurred at night. The darkness seemed to be a safe haven for the advances of these terror mongers and, believe me, they took full advantage of it. By daylight I would go venturing about. The people neither perched in alleyways nor swaggered so boldly as in the menacing city nor, of course, was there the crowding. I imagined that there were less antics due to the surrender forced upon these troops by the imperious powers of nature that abound all around us. However, they knew as did I, that I was not properly equipped to disappear. Where was I to go, after all, hemmed in by the rugged steeps of nature? Yes, they seemed to show the proper stature of presence and I am sure their checkpoints were well established. For instance, on one of my many walks I would encounter an occasional man, woman, or family traversing my path.Well, what was I to think? They knew and I knew, our situation as well as our manners. We would nod and smile in complicity with one another. At other times I would sneak off into the woods itching to get clear of the human race. Tired of being the axis of this supersensible world, I would wind through the maze of trees. But, alas, they would ferret me out with the uncanny technology at their disposal. Oh dear, my determined pigeons of progress, I would remark in disbelief. From this great kingdom a heap of voices eagerly yakked. Sweeping the superhighway, my unseen darlings?

I would challenge. But, of course, their talk was of nothing, so they wished me to believe, of nothing at all they would drone, shooing me away as if I was of no consequence. Meanwhile, I could hear the rubbing of their hands conceiving of new mischief, like the happy winner of a poker game. What a duplicitous nature we have, my heroes, I would loudly reflect.

No, it was no use trying to avoid the others. Knowing that I was being monitored in this physical isolation gave me no comfort whatsoever. I began to conceive of my reentry into the populated world. My bank account was dwindling away. As luck would have it, the nearest city was a gambling town as well. Though a different terrain the game was the same. The game, that is, of radiant fortune through divine benevolence. But then, so was my predicament. Meanwhile, I couldn't very well summon the courage to camp out with these tormentors. My mind was being continually challenged. I needed the luxury of a prepared meal evening if it was being poisoned by who knows what. Yes, Ineeded to keep light and mobile, not weighing myself down with any additional hardships in this scramble that had consumed my life. The fixed, rapt attention of all others almost approached a state of prayer and I would have to respond in kind to survive my ordeal. Hush now, I would remind myself, again and again. Things continued and I continued to burrow in as well. Madly seeking reason as our forefathers sought fire I continued to poke into this wilderness of exchange. Examining a strand of hair or the lint of a sweater would take painstaking hours. Clues to this imprisonment must lay somewhere, I begged. These mountains that were once so very friendly had now become a sanctuary for remote hordes of screaming voices. From an idle bough something of a toy bird would shriek as in some demonic mythology. Playing with harpies, I would feebly cry into this land of Nod. I began to feel a little like a past acquaintance, a woman I barely once knew, who leapt like a lemming into the sea's rocks below, poor girl. But she was as mad and disfigured as could be imagined while I was as lucid as light. Such nature and nurture may account for her dark times, bless her. However, she was simply a helpless case while I lay a thousand miles this other side of angel's platinum markers. No, I could see surely enough! I was suffering from a fate never written, from a shadow without words. I was the last hanging claw of reality, the running light. As I stole through this web of appearances even the clouds above would amass like some blessed nimbus, shrouding me as a shield. If only my flight was swift enough! If only I could escape from this blinding, dark crystal! But I only race forth, the sthenic wand upon me, the star's flint flashing between my eyes.

While packing my car I noticed a young woman putting a call into the authorities from a public telephone. Her forehead seemed to express nervous puzzlement. Perhaps, it was evil badgering one of the countless P.P.A. at their outposts. One would have to possess quite a stagnant mind to ignore the obvious discord of every word, gesture, and deed that lay like mines of good and evil in my path. And, well, that glimmer of light sliding across the eye was as good as any tongue-in-cheek.

I quickly stopped off the road to purchase coffee, then I crawled back into my car. Again the suspicious stillness haunted the landscape and inhabited the expressive lines of all other faces culminating appreciably in the flecks of the iris. Little else seemed to be happening. Of course, they had ample time to make preparations for my departure, no matter what direction I might venture. As before they simply didn't wish to call attention to themselves. All action depended upon this masquerade of indifference. Of that, I was well aware!

Split by the sun, a few clouds dragged their shadows over this hunting plain. I was no more than an hour from my destination when I was jolted by this sensation of heat emanating from my seat once again. The radio was on low and for some distant reason, some small possibility, I suppose, I turned it up wondering if I might be able to alter the flow of this oppressive heat. As the song grew louder I could hear in the muffled background, camouflaged by the tune itself, the horrible declaration that I would never forget.

"They're killing you with ultrasound," the voice warned over and over, "they're killing you with ultrasound!" Stunned by this disclosure and the rising heat I pulled over. All speech was strangled by this form of speed.

I dashed out of my car popping the hood to get a better look at this device; the one pointed out to me by the stranger, whom I had helped start his car some time ago. And I wondered, again, whether or not he was from this inner sect, the P.P.A., following an esoteric lead, or from these evil others. I knew that sound given a certain frequency could heat up soft tissue but I couldn't theorize how this was being empowered and focused. A part of me dismissed it as implausible nonsense, but my sensate self reminded me of the hideous affects I had experienced now on two separate occasions. I looked around at the engine confoundedly and finally yanked some wires from the radio.

Climbing back into my car I felt a little dizzy from all of the diabolical possibilities. Racing along the road, I placed all hope upon my new destination, as if it was to be some final refuge. After a while I began to dry spit and babble with the renewed sensation of heat and mental acceleration. Fortunately, a restaurant lay up ahead. I pulled over, ejecting myself from this oven cooking me inside out. Food and the help of the P.P.A. was that for which I longed. Perhaps 'they' were sneaking into my system an antidote to these fatal waves of vibration. I was almost certain they would have control over the restaurant. Leaving my car unlocked, I scurried toward the restaurant. There was no reason to secure my car now while people tampered with it as they pleased, and so I left the windows open as well. Upon entering the café I felt immediate relief. There was good-natured laughter, the smell of home cooking, and the delightful checkered table cloths reminded me gracefully of my first love's summer dress.I sat down at the counter alone not wishing to indulge in any more feinted scripts. I was content being the mere passive recipient of the joyful exchanges taking place. But as I looked casually about me, in between studying the menu, I noticed a few characters of a more somber nature. Suddenly I caught a glimpse of my brother. Not my brother exactly, for he was well disguised. Nevertheless, something inside me knew that this was him - his posture, his glasses, his gestures, and his expressions. I quickly looked away so as not to let on to our complicity, and I glared appreciatively at the pies in the cabinet windows. I felt ashamed at being in this merciless situation and imperiling others but what could I do? It was out of my power and this, I am certain, he understood.I casually looked again, catching his eyes, and then I looked away marveling not only at his disguise but the power of recognition at my disposal. No doubt, this power privileged upon me through love and the mystifying properties of shared blood. Knowing my brother and his sense of humor he was, perhaps, plying my own. What healthy medicine! I thought. Why, he is both mocking my earlier disguise of a nose and glasses while at the same time hiding his own identity. Killing two birds with one stone, eh? Bravo! I quietly muttered, contriving of a way myself to acknowledge him without raising suspicion. The waitress arrived and I placed my order not giving away the felicitous mood brought about by the present circumstances. One could never be too careful, I silently chimed, recalling the dermatologist's motto. My spirit seemed to glow from deep within as I thought about such clandestine confrontations of the French underground. I put my little finger in my ear and jiggled it as my father used to do. This would surely be a private association of which only we were aware. All in all, it blended very coolly and insidiously with the drama surrounding us. In fact, it was shortly thereafter acknowledged by his cough. My appetite grew as little rushes of excitement passed through me from my family company. However, my happiness was dampened somewhat by the disappointment of our great and necessary distance. A tear started to come but I counseled myself into obedience thinking of more fortunate times. As I paid the cashier I raised my little finger and, once again, wiggled it for a few telling seconds. I told the employee 'thank you' with just the smallest note of inflection and gave a friendly wink. Then letting out a fateful sigh as I opened the lower half of the Dutch door, I exited with reborn hope and with prayers for these angels helping me. Upon entering the city I pledged to myself to give more effort in controlling my fears. I reasoned out of instinct that I must further adapt or perish. I must put away all maudlin outbursts and hysteria. I must keep body and soul together, as they say. Through thick and thin, my compatriots would not desert me. Even if there was an unsettling fury of traffic buzzing around me now did I not owe my conformity to their battle plans, whatever they might be? Hadn't they, for the moment, succeeded in preventing anymore of this ultrasound campaign? Perhaps, they had even removed the demonic apparatus from my car, while I was preoccupied with their charms in the restaurant.Regrettably, the hotel I had checked into did not have a pool. This would translate into walking as my means of exercise. In fact, I began to mull over the possibility of selling my car thereby prolonging my freedoms. My time went by uneventful enough. I had become habituated to the usual ploys and pranks of my surveillance. I would scamper to and fro with wild abandon untouched by the unusual proceedings around me. My attendants began to use their access to superannuated radio communications, apparently useful enough for the time being. I became immune not only to these security officers covering the casinos but to car alarms being set off at critical junctures. Such were their methods of announcing my whereabouts. National flags designating the ports of the P.P.A. allegiance flew proudly as I passed various checkpoints. The coughing never stopped as well. With each block it seemed a new stranger would greet me with this peculiar salutation. The one armed bandits were calibrated in rhythm to their infrasonic correspondence. Every ringing machine would address me with idle pleasantries or, occasionally, with fatal threats. As there was nothing that I could do, I accepted it as well as one could. After all, I was nothing more than a fugitive of sorts by now. I continued to burn off some of the residual vigor left by their drug potions by walking and occupying myself with harmless games. For example, one morning I would recite every word that I could think of beginning with the letter 'e.' As fast as I could I would mutter; exit, elastic, egress, erupt, entrance, and on and on. Finally, after having suffered palpitations from this exuberance I would stop. The next morning would bear the same practice using a different letter. I longed desperately to disappear from the frantic public. Everywhere people walked in haste and aimlessness. When I would shut myself up in my hotel room the forces at work would continue hammering me. As if my solitude was not enough they would beat me up with lethal suggestions. Either crooning for me to jump out of the hotel window or alternately wooing me with their praise and affection, they continued without let. My life had become a nightly war between love and death. What was to become of me, rowing in these slave quarters of their madness? Would this rain of pattering whispers never cease? The more that I thought about it in my confusion both evil and good now seemed to mimic one another. In fact, they grew like branches from a common trunk. Why, they even played with one another, depended upon each other for this ruse to continue. Who was I to them? Only middleman, a master of nothing, subject to the pull of these uncontrollable forces. No man is safe from this world! I would cry and reason thus. Hasn't our fate been written long ago in the chemistry of the universe? We are simply the muttering attributes of our seasons. Meanwhile, we assume responsibility and act accordingly. Hadn't I demonstrated this through thick and thin? Why? Because that, too, is written in our blood. But in the end, before we shut our eyes one last time, we must know that things could not have been any different. Each of our stories is as old as time. But these are old postulates, I would curse, and come to think of it I no longer feel that they are necessarily true nor do I really care. No, man is just a passing mood. That's as far as I can go. I'm sure that we would all agree that the mind is a lonesome trick. Though it burns like a hot star, the body supplies us with all the pleasure and wisdom one needs to know. But what is the meaning of all of these idlers everywhere I go and the sacrilege of this invasion? Why me? It must be some mythic form of fate like seeing your face in a river, and such a treacherous performance must yield this inescapable following! Yes, I struggled. What else could explain the nature of this sordid venture? Again, these demons waited for no response but delightfully chattered among themselves as if at a tea party.

III

Another week had passed but time no longer had any meaning. The poison was being given to me more frequently and it was becoming increasingly difficult to get anything done. As I was no closer to ascertaining its origin, I was forced to walk the plank as best I could. My body was weak and nervous, my brain raged on at breakneck speed, then would slump into a state of exhaustion. I bought a self developing camera. However, I was unable to put together a clean package of goods against all of these forces and I became more lethargic in my defeat. I hopped into my car and drove out of the city anxious to escape, if only for the moment, its tedious amusements. A wave of nausea soon came over me. I pulled to the side of the road to get a grip on myself and to retrieve the recorder that had slid off the seat into a pile of paper cups and upon my clipboard filled with license plate numbers. I had to muster all of my strength for clarity through this aching pain. I flipped on the recorder and I spoke the date and hour. Then I described my bodily sensations and gave a summation of my ordeal. I played it back to ensure that it worked properly. I wasn't at all certain if anybody would be interested in it or if it was safe or necessary in light of my situation. My voice was completely unrecognizable and I wondered very seriously if it was me at all. It faltered and groaned from some deep burning well inside me as though I was heavily sedated.

How I longed for a return to the simple joy that was my life and the smallest of love's forms. What I wouldn't do for a laughing swim; to think of my former love, the color of her face before she slept, or a cheerful meal with a friend or a stranger!

However, the chase continued as cars fanned out about me in deliberate waves. Never quite clear or on my own. Always caught up within eyesight. Everywhere people raced about devouring the horizon. They even went so far as to place idle motorists in the middle of nowhere or simply picking their teeth in the parking lots. As usual the public telephones were all occupied by these masqueraders and collaborators. The great wave of eerie light continued to fall as all of these seekers roamed without their wits, hard on the prowl. I ran into a country store and bought an apple. Then I trotted back hopping in my car without noticing any customers glancing my way. I consumed this little morning repast with no appreciable difference of feeling. Besides how would they conspire to drug me not knowing what I would choose to eat or to drink?

However, this notion failed to assuage

my fears as I only had to recall the undeniable sensations my body had experienced on numerous occasions Looking into the car's mirror I could make out my pupils dilated from this aphrodisiac. Venus in heels, eh, I smirked. Perhaps the clerk had affected a chemical reaction of sorts or some invisible gas was being exploded from within my car. If the latter was true its only evidence was the sharp crack of my dash. I didn't expect to get away scot-free from their shenanigans but their clever methods still perplexed me. Like playing with a puppet, I groaned. I looked down and I noticed my checkbook sticking halfway out of the pocket of the door. It's curious, I thought, what is going to happen to me, unable to work and exhausting my checking and saving accounts. That this can't continue indefinitely is a sure thing. A state of privation is certainly peeking from just around the corner. But wait! Perhaps this Public Protection Agency has some plan to secretly deposit money into my accounts. Money, let's say, I continued on with impeccable reasoning, that might be pledged by this agency. If it was in well-measured denominations it might be entirely possible. I checked my last balance and collated it. There was a definite mismatch, although it was only modestly in my favor. Come to think of it, wasn't it peculiar that a federal marshal had entered the bank from behind me a few months ago. And I sat in the stupor that this fact produced for the next five minutes unable to fathom all of the subtle coincidences that were gradually coming to light. I motored back toward town with my entourage pondering my situation. Even though the car was like a good friend and a form of refuge from this dizzying world I realized that my travels had been costly. Yes, I concurred with myself, selling the car would be my only recourse in this steep ride, this hell of ambiguity. How long, after all, could I suffer postponement of my financial affairs? No, the enormity of this state of affairs insisted upon the mandate that 'they' were quite well-prepared to redress me for my substantial losses! But then, who was I to assume a full knowledge of these two colliding forces, so at odds, yet oftentimes, mimicking one another to a hair. Look on the bright side, I reminded myself. You're a bit of a gypsy, a tramp, in fact! You won't have any trouble carrying your luggage in your heart and upon the end of a stick. They've certainly picked the wrong man to pursue. Why, with my convoluted travels I would give them all vertigo. From now on just the sweet earth mixed with the simple music of my soul, I snickered. Who, after all, needs these gadabouts? No, to be sure, I was destined for a walkabout!

Suddenly there was an explosion, like a rifle shot. I calmly looked into my rearview mirror assuming the suspense of an amused audience toward this concussive sound. I could see a man, seemingly startled reach to unlatch the hood of his car. He looked around dumbfounded, then lifted the hood, smoke steaming up into the air. I couldn't help but notice that he wore a pager and I swiftly transcribed its meaning. Like a fine performance he was imitating me at the origins of my plight. The fumbling technologist, pager tucked into belt. Back to the future, eh! Were they expecting me to wince with pain and incredulity again? But such appearances insulted me and only made me desperate with laughter. I was, by now, so immune to their agenda of deceit, these impish lords and ladies of my undoing, that I became arrogant in my enmity. Why I'll throw him lock, stock, and barrel into the jaws of death, I moaned weakly. I clutched my abdomen, hit by the ultrasound again, and I laughed myself into a fit of weeping. If this keeps up, I mumbled, I'll choke on my own phlegm and we can all make a short day of it!

This glowing farce precipitated my sense of humor. I began to consider wrapping myself in ace bandages like a mummy and walking the streets as the invisible man. How else could I show these failed actors to what lengths they were contributing to my death. How feckless had their performances become with time?

But I decided that this was mere hyperbole. Yes, this was the same excessive attitude I had born witness to just the other day. A man had walked by with a brown paper bag over his head. No doubt he was from this party of lowbrows ridiculing my own previous disguise. What a poor showing! Who cares what these pests think, I uttered with disgust. I'll don my limited disguise and make that due, I thought with final determination, and I put on my glasses and nose. Keep an even keel and maintain your reasonable presence — dignity, my good friend. But remember, you don't want to shortchange the public altogether of some vital entertainment in these dark times.

Particularly, for those that are still caring enough to carry the torch for you, lighting your way. On the other hand avoid extravagance at all costs, I reminded myself. I arrived back at my hotel room, nerves on edge. It was a commonplace condition by now but there was no getting used to it. Thoughts of the agency's divine intervention into my sad financial situation reappeared. In this connection I raced down to the casino to place a bet, my first such bet in this gambling charade. Perhaps this was the means whereby my fate would be changed, I thought with great expectancy. The dealer showed a 'stiff' and I 'doubled down' with happy anticipation. I noticed another player giving me a sly look. The next thing that I knew the dealer was collecting my bet. No doubt this other gambler was my adversary and the P.P.A. was powerless to affect a change of fortune in his presence. I looked at him briefly and I shook from his cold, gray appearance. Sickened by this thug and the gambling ambience in general, I went directly up to my room for some more thoughtful considerations.

I paced the room with the television on, then turned it off again, bothered by the noise. Dreamily through the window I looked down at the dead end alleyway toward which my unseen visitants had beckoned me to jump a few nights ago. I could almost feel myself falling and screaming through midair when I turned away not wanting any further to recall the night. Unable to face people for the moment I called room service and ordered a meal. It arrived shortly thereafter as if it had been pre-prepared. I ate what I could of it and I lay back surrendering to my fatigue. Communications returned. From what I could gather by their modulation of alarm and the content of their message it was the P.P.A. 'You're sick, go to the E.R.,' it repeated in a solicitous voice. Suddenly I felt as fragile as this house of cards in which I lay. Frightened by their urgency I picked up the telephone book and searched for the address of the nearest hospital. But my mind was reeling with worry and in my confusion over what would be the nearest hospital I was forced to call the hotel desk. No time to linger, I thought, beseeched by the instructive tone of the P.P.A. I drove by the clerk's directions with as much attention as I could bring to bear in my fear. Breathing was difficult and I felt as though I was going to lose control of my bowels. However, when I began speaking to the triage nurse at the emergency room I was at a loss for words. Did they not know that I was coming? They must be aware, I reprimanded myself, and I continued to invent some vague form of symptoms. I sheepishly muttered the words now worried about the various parties sitting in the waiting room. Again I wasn't able to determine what side they represented. As a result I remained indefinite and equivocal telling her that I had a fever and that I was a bit diaphoretic. Hemming and hawing, laying out the tedious network of lies, in short, I prevaricated from within the abstractedness I found sitting among me. It seemed as though an eternity had passed before they were through collecting urine and blood and checking my vital signs. I felt foolish standing there in my gown, cold as ice, wondering what it was that might have gone wrong. Was it a misjudgment, perhaps, on the dosage of the medication being given to me? I wondered. Finally a doctor arrived telling me that it was probably a virus of some sort. That was all! I left feeling betrayed. Had they by some mysterious means neutralized this danger? Who could stop this tympanic symphony caged within my brain? I was in need of having my skull stapled shut!

Returning to my empty room I tossed the car keys on the dresser and flopped down upon the bed. A moment passed, a dreamy lull, and the communications oozed, once again, through the floorboards and vents. 'You're sick, go to the E.R!' With frightful shock I began to examine my own pulse and I felt suddenly very queasy. What was I to do? Had I gone to the wrong hospital? I certainly did not want to take the chance of disobeying this command and jeopardize my life. My spiritual resources weren't exhausted yet.

Although sometimes, I confess, I had implored for an easy way out, my instinct was to live! I desperately tore through the telephone book and I discovered the name and address of another hospital. As the front desk was no longer a trustworthy source I used my own cunning to reach the hospital. After some difficulty finding it, I walked in and described the problem as before. Again time passed and the same diagnosis was spoken. Tired and confused I returned to the hotel determined to get some rest. The entire night had passed while I flitted about to these directives. I coaxed myself to sleep with the promise that tomorrow would be the day of my departure. The power of my will, my intent, and my aspirations had usually clung to memory for some saving contrast of new and old worlds. But this time there was no way around their tricks. With thoughts of my old familiar world I turned exhausted upon the pillow. Longing for a path of reunion, I fell into a dreamless sleep. The next morning I washed and packed, anxious for new beginnings. Now was not the time to hang on to possessions. This entire program governing my life was no more, nor less, a plea predicated upon survival alone! It was time to return to the woods and water for a spell before my favorite time of year, autumn. But would I be able to settle down anywhere in this raging climate of nerves, speed, and indifference? Questions kept coming without answers but I couldn't shut them off. Wasn't life worth more than riches anyway? Wasn't I, in fact, a man rich with memory? Hadn't I worn my heart on my sleeve and thus far received so many endearing benefits? I began to count my blessings through the present mire of my life. A used car dealership lay up ahead. I figured that they would give me a good price knowing the many dangers I'd been through, the anguish I'd suffered day in and day out. Certain that one lot would be much like another I settled for proximity. I made no bones about haggling over the price. Besides I was spent after last night's leap into confusion. To my surprise they offered me only half of what it was worth. Still, it seemed like a considerable sum compared to the few dollars I had remaining. The invaluable time it would buy shone before me like a reprieve from this quickening pursuit. No, I was in no position to barter, and this they knew. If the P.P.A. couldn't manage to squeeze together a more earnest amount than this let it be on their shoulders, their conscience, I reasoned. Furthermore, what had I to lose, I declared. I have not only next to nothing but have been robbed of peace of mind altogether. There was no making sense of this turbulence. Has any man suffered such a giddy maze of human activity and insouciance, I wondered. Had I ever heard of such a thing? Could one ever possibly learn of such things if all traces of the victim disappeared through their methods. Could one stay alive to combat these forces? Or was it only a matter of time before one took his own life? There were, of course, the tales of suicide with which I was familiar. Perhaps, they too, had been made a mockery of by these same bloodhounds, witnessed the haughty day to day hammer blows, and the fearful clash of so many lost, impervious others from within this same complete solitude. We drew up the papers and I signed at the designated areas, glad almost, to be rid of it. Why, I'll make tracks with my feet. I left some of my belongings in the car telling them that I was in a hurry to make preparations for my new job back east and that I would return to collect them later this afternoon. Kind and patient of me, I thought, to act out these small logistical niceties like a normal man. Yes, there was sympathy in their eyes, no doubt, for knowing the hardships that I'd endured and the integrity with which I proceeded. I asked the salesman if he would be kind enough to drive me to a bank honoring their check. He agreed. I snatched the one bag I had packed at the hotel from the trunk together with a heavy jacket, and climbed unsteadily into his awaiting car. Feeling bereaved by the shelter and mobility it had seen me through I nodded goodbye to my car and felt, once more, estranged from the society in which I had lived. Hitch-hiking was certainly out of the question. I'd never be able to catch a ride with my unprecedented status. The walk to the mountain village was too unkindly far. Moreover, there was no alternate back road, other than the super highway. No, the bus would have to do.

IV

I arrived in the early afternoon. It was a town with which I was very familiar but now it appeared to be no more than a cast of tourists on a movie set for the 'Ol West. Everything seemed strange, an anachronism of the nineteenth century. I immediatelyinstalled myself at a bed and breakfast lodging in order to stow my gear. There was a large registration book, embossed with gold lettering, for the clientele to date and sign as a form of record and amusement. I peered at a number of the names laughing at the inventiveness of these good people. Why, names that could either follow a count or blend into the cedar work of this place ever so perfectly. Some just stood out garishly, some were quite comical, and others were of a foreign flavor.

Some were scrawled by a cramped hand, others generously flowing, some grotesquely unique, while still others were illegible or easily recitative. Once more I couldn't comprehend the enormity of this deceit. In this atmosphere of great, grandmother's house I was feeling like a part of a museum, a character from the past century atmosphere of great, grandmother's house I was feeling like a part with no future. Stuck fast within this eternal historic moment, however, I felt no different really than what had been the present day to me at one time. The same markers flanked me, that of gossip and indifference, but the speed of things had waned mildly. This agreed with me. Nevertheless, dazed by something of an awkward premonition, I pedaled my way to the second floor between my persecutors and protectors. I sat upon the bed, my mind teeming with impish thoughts, and stared at the washbowl that lay upon the dresser. Nervously squeezing the crocheted blanket between my thumb and index finger, I began to tune into another frequency. From within this new form of media two distinct voices arose, friends of mine. I must tell you, I didn't know whether to laugh or to cry! I was beside myself with joy. They summarized their position above me telling me that it was simply too dangerous for them to appear. No, this was their only possible medium of communications, they assured me, and sent their deepest love. Then they proceeded to appeal to my sense of humor. Stand up and mimic us, they taunted, laughing and giggling like a couple of schoolboys from out of *Huck Finn*. I complied with great enthusiasm! Standing there as though the accomplished diseur, I filled the air with first one, then the other's gestures. Congratulated from moment to moment by their riotous laughter, I picked away at these resemblances.

Finally, after this exhilarating performance among my loving company they informed me that it was time to say goodbye and quickly exited from my senses. I felt somewhat rejuvenated but saddened by their disappearance. And so I sat in the shadows of loneliness with a heavy heart from their departure. Perhaps I was thinking of nothing at all or I was merely feeding myself in pity the axiom that I must be, by now, their idol if strength resides in suffering. But alas, I stirred from these painful depths and escaped into the street to play at my first day of being the tramp. It was proving to be one fine day! A fine trail of song accompanied me as I strode through this village. Difficult to imagine in this dry air and radiant light, nonetheless, not too far from here lay the history of cannibalism in a deepening snow. In contrast, I celebrated my expansive mood with a few well-chosen smiles. No doubt, the cheerful residua left me from a visit with my dear friends upstairs. As if to declare independence day to all kindred souls, I stepped into a coffee house. But I started to feel hemmed in, stifled. I couldn't help but feel something new and frightening slip into this merry mood of mine. What kind of mysticism was this? I asked myself. Undaunted I placed my order. The woman serving me showed not the slightest trace of emotion. To the unobserving eye this could lead to undeserved complacency. However, this was a different matter altogether. This otherwise common response now smacked of deliberation, of forethought. My suspicions were confirmed in her next act for she made the mistake of discarding the first cup that she had withdrawn from the dispenser. Poor training or a bad case of nerves, I thought to myself. Well, her cards had been played. Though I marveled at the cute innocence with which she resumed her activities, I dashed out congratulating myself on my new discovery of their methods. I felt my body tighten now rid of the innocence of the day and put myself on full alert. Stalwart and lean I marched on, a small victory of insight at hand, prepared to walk one thousand miles if necessary. Yes, though hard pressed, I had permitted her side glance to serve as an apology and without condemning her I departed. In high fashion now I walked, eyes toward the sky, oblivious toward any obsequious gestures from the well-meaning but befuddled help of the Public Protection Agency. We were, after all, allowed our failures in such colossal confusion, I confessed rather magnanimously. However, all of a sudden I felt that my philosophy of quiet and circumspect desperation had now become greatly magnified. To get away, run at any cost, why it would be anyone's natural impulse. Surely there would be good with the bad, I meditated. No matter what was to come my way could I not, within limits, manage the part of the stoic? Hadn't I always survived on this formula of instinct and learned to bend with the river? The principle thing was the less to be responsible for the better. This denuding of oneself was the key with which to bide time, or so I reasoned. And the result was to divide myself equally between the paraphernalia of a daypack and the blue, mountain sky. All things considered what dangers was I overlooking? How was I to muddle my case so that 'they' would fall into hopelessness when regarding my situation and my life's acquaintances? How to make them surrender with my obscurity in this fencing and weaving from town to town, week to week, month to month? But soon after these ruminations I stumbled upon a display window of camping equipment. In the glass I could make out my strange, pale reflection, blanched with fear. It seemed as though I was wearing the scars of my crises. From the corner of my eyes I took notice of those around me and walked on rather sheepishly. Then I abruptly turned to brazenly retrace my footsteps. Of course, my purchase and hence, my plans, would be revealed at once. It was impossible to hide my intentions. I purchased a sleeping bag and a daypack. Both were immoderately priced showing, I imagine, the P.P.A.'s vexation with me for trying to go it alone. Evidently greater mobility thus made it more difficult for them in their task. Such intuition was well illustrated by little expressions - the heavy pause and slow packaging of my purchase, the slightly raised eyebrow of the clerk. I continued down the road in the opposite direction from my lodgings leaving the nineteenth century behind me. The scent of the forest burned my nostrils as I entered the wooded park by a small lake. The palpitating woods seem to shiver from their roots bruised by cold water springs. Their burning incense had sent the nymph and satyr to sleep in the naked shade. Humming a tune to keep away the evil spirits I followed a trail to the water.

Dappling sunlight striped my vision and the heavy mascara of shadows mottled the forest's floor. Under the lash of the sun, bearing my carapace for worldly goods, I advanced toward the wimpling lake. I was navigating my way, it seemed, by magnetic waves of sirens. Yes, beneath this flaming eye I was finally becoming the profound pleasure of my legs. Like all beasts I was surrendering to the simple travail of their daily path walking the walk of thewanderer. At the water's edge I sat down lotus style and began to quietly laugh, keeping it the secret it should naturally be. Then the damning wind sprang up behind me and the inventions of my brain quickened into a chorus:

Such are the little abortuses of our spirit,
That inhabit a backstage of gloved shadows
And stillborn cries;
Where unspeakable terrors rain down
Rehearsals for future performance,
Braiding humor with the hangman's rope.

I captured the importance of these lines though I didn't quite know what they meant. I would have to create a diary in the air, untraceable to all but the sight of angels.

As though in a trance, yet alert to the smallest of details, I watched the lake with its tiny bursts of white water. My, I thought, how far had things come in the frantic exodus of these last months. I lay back, my mind trailing off into a plume of ecstatic intangibles. Bruised by melancholy, under the rigorous light, I listened carefully now to the P.P.A. fixing its transmissions upon me. "We're giving you your medicine," they whispered. 'Bleed me, I am saltwater running into the sea,' I softly lisped, and numb I finally succumbed and dozed off. When I awoke dusk was settling into night. Again, for the moment, my anguish was behind me. I was hungry and, what with my exercise and fasting, slimming down a bit. My nourishment seemed to be coming from the air as did everything else — my medication, my communications, and so on. It seemed to dictate not only the larger movements and direction of my course but controlled the very weather of my soul as well. For my moods were, once again, coming and going like the troughs of hot and cold in a summer's orchard. Fevers and sweats of ardor broke my stride and bent the wildflowers of my slender ideas. I wandered back to town. People, as usual, walked past me as if I was invisible.

My mind began to speed up and I lost myself to incoherent babble, muttering curses under my breath and storming about in all directions. Struck by this ultrasound again I scrambled away from town. At such times I needed to be alone to control this innermost sensation of falling forever from the face of the earth. The quiddity of these ulcerating vibrations made my blood run cold. I would hold onto myself in order to calm down. I smoked a cigarette, cupping it so that nobody could detect me in the glowing, palpable darkness beneath the trees. There I sat, humming to the pinball labyrinth of my world, tinkering with childhood memory. Finally, walking out of my shelter, I turned toward the sky as toward a premonition. Ah! Rewarded at the end of this eternal day by the moon! I declared.

I suddenly longed to kiss the full flanks of its tender flame and to softly trace the bloodlines of the human race so that I might calm the flubuggery of my wagging tongue. Just to clap for the moon amidst this woody parish and to momentarily quench my thirst with such sweets for the forsaken. Yes, I wanted to kneel down, like the parturition of the damned, struck dumb by day's lightening. Wasn't it time for some welcome clearing? To just take a monk's respite from this touch and go, these synaptic alarms. Pounding out a choir of tears, stuttering at the forgotten world, a mere ventriloquist filled with speed and pain, I wished one last time. 'Oh, my gentle fawn give to me the saving covenant of one small kiss! Oh, Claire! I was your disciple of tenderness and the wind. Forgive me and my absence of courage. This flood of tears seemed to wash away my cares. I felt immeasurable love for this stubborn paper-chain of struggling life. I rose humbled from the experience and hobbled along the roadside past the trees. It was sharply lit up now and then by the stalking automobiles of these two parties.

I could not bring myself to eat among these people and I bought a jar of nuts and a bottle of mineral water to satisfy my hunger and thirst. At home, sweet home, I decided to let the Public Protection Agency and my fateful nemesis both hear a softer side of my life. It had lately become too much riddled with the spoils of survival - frantic displays and moody sentiments. I opened a small volume of poetry and very carefully read in a soft, caressing voice to my captors words that had befriended me through these troubled times. At thoughtful moments, I would pause to tell these silent listening ears of my life. I would describe to them of the first instances in my childhood when a loving nana would read to my beautiful sister and I by the cool breezes of a fan. Over the porch and through the screen door the scent of red roses would mingle sweetly with her lilac.

How new worlds and bright pictures would light up before my eyes! I was privileged to enter one fairy tale after another. The soft and calm flow of her voice as pleasing as the sound of water breathed life into each and every character. I read on feeling the deep pleasure of sharing confidences until I finally turned on my side and fell to dreamless sleep. The next morning I awoke and showered. Refreshed and looking expectantly toward my morning coffee, I sauntered downtown whistling and chirping like the scraping blue joys.

Though it was still early the streets bristled with the energy of more new recruits. I walked up and down the streets entertaining myself as well as others in the same way as the pleasant night before. My pocket edition of King Lear had finally come in handy. I would spout out an occasional line or verse and then tear it like a dead leaf from its weak binding only to deposit it in the trash. But before too long my voice would sink and from the haunting backcloth of the forest voices would yawn with derision. As from some great and distant bellows this 'windmill,' as I referred to it, would begin to turn and graze my ears with wavering chorus. 'No body so light as yours, my dear Mercury,' I would utter in self encouragement and revolt. But, of no fault of my own, my pace would quicken to accommodate these communications and, alas, I would be off trotting into the horizon before I knew it. It was, after all, the only way. Practiced again and again, I tore these demons from my side with the quick and able, marching comradery of deepest soul. My voice seemed to oscillate from the vigor and punch of this survival. Being of some shyness I could no longer suffer this public forum. Slowly, I wandered out of town toward this child-sized lake. Smartly dressed in a crumpled, blue blazer and a beret I shuttled to the park once again. There I sat, expelled from the nineteenth century by a bunch of merciless bloodhounds. Plans of escape began to form in myrestless mind. I would wait until evening and hop a train. I wouldn't be easily found out, I reflected, if I was to jump off in the middle of nowhere! Eternities seemed to pass before darkness fell. I began to fuel my courage with memories.

Finally, I heard the train that lay in wait start to disengage. Its steel wheels thundered with a horrendous clatter and screech. My cowardice began to grow as I picked myself up and began to shamble uncertainly by the moving cars. Suddenly I recalled a vagrant, like myself, that had been brought into a hospital where I had once worked. Though I never saw him I had overheard the doctors laboriously discussing his several injuries in graphic detail. He had been accidentally crushed by the weight of one of these 'iron horses.' No, it was too risky for a similar fate. I could imagine the gross amputations, my limbs sundered from my torso like butter. I slunk down, dizzy upon my knees, to the stationary earth and I looked up into the sky for consolation from the soft, bridal eye of the moonlight. Something quieted from within, and from the fluted wind of the trees, I could hear one thousand echoes imploring 'we love you, we love you,' This insistent skirl piped in the nourishment that had steadied my flesh-eaten soul more than once, allowing me to further drift, "scarce half-made up"*(Shakespeare)* along the rim of the world.

V

Some time passed and I became tired of being landlocked by hill and dale. My desire rose toward the aromatic wonders of the sea and the liberty of an open horizon. There an equilibrium might be granted me by the supernal mix of light and water. Who knows, I thought, perhaps I would be in time for the solar eclipse and honor the predestined meeting with my old hitch-hiking friend. By noon the following day I had been transported by bus to the valley and state capitol. There I made a transfer to the next coach that would take me through the dry, uneventful valley, then wind, like a saw-toothed blade, toward the southern coast. Apparently, one more transfer would see me to my final destination which lay about one half hour from the country's border. The monotony of scenery and stifling heat had me longing, all the more, for the coastal flora and fauna, and the ocean breezes. I must have dozed off for about an hour from the toll of all of these irregular events and my erratic patterns of sleep. Upon waking I noticed that the scenery had not changed a bit. Perhaps, I thought, the P.P.A. had examined me and given me a dose of my medicine as I slept. There was a discernible difference in bodily sensation. Nothing, mind you, that had not happened to me before. Nonetheless, my thoughts started to race along with no object in mind. My voice box chattered away nervously. Swallowing became more difficult and frequent. I had to make a conscious effort to stifle the noticeable display of energy coursing through my body. Moreover, my stomach was gnawing at me and my body began to burn. I placed a hand on my stomach, rocking mildly to and fro, to suppress the pain of the ultrasound and to quiet my mewling like a child. Fortunately, I was wearing sunglasses so that nobody could witness my pain through the reflex of my eyes. "Lie back" I heard the voices intone, "We're giving you medicine." I complied, but had begun to question which side had made this mandate. I noticed a man typing at his laptop computer. My communications began to scamper like the wings of an insect. Could this be the orgin of the assault upon me or some form of hypnotism, I marveled in my state of shock. But it didn't really matter; I was too damaged now to care. It was no good! I could not suppress the pain eating away at me and my worry about physically erupting had me paralyzed with fear. Finally after an unimaginable length of time, the bus pulled off the highway. A few passengers readied themselves to disembark. Very thoughtfully I had taken my baggage aboard. 'Thank goodness' I muttered, and I slipped off the bus with them. The symptoms now rather mysteriously subsided as though I was suddenly out of range. The air felt pleasing.

I spied a restaurant not far away and decided to treat myself to a cool drink. After all, I was in no hurry and it was impossible to stay put in the close quarters of the bus.

I consumed some fruit and voraciously gulped at my iced tea. I was beginning to feel safe when I noticed her, a dear relative of mine, an angel. She and a few of her friends strolled by with big smiles on their shining faces. Though she was disguised so superbly, the interpretive powers of blood and recognition once again prevailed. So easily was I able to breach her distorting guise that I consequently became quite anxious. I simply didn't want her involved at all in this dangerous climate. She was so young and full of promise in contrast to this impending doom surrounding me that I was, of course, afraid for her wellbeing. I knew that she meant well but seemed to play at this drama too lightheartedly as is customary of youth. The next time I saw her with my peripheral vision I subtly raised my hand to my head and tapped once and once only.

At this she suddenly departed and I reprimanded myself for risking her life with such a patent form of communication. Abruptly following her exit the windows of the restaurant began to rattle as if from a quake or sonic boom. I felt the same phenomena rise from within my body. I sat there numb with fear.

Again the windows shook as from a violent shock and the rumble of heavy trucks boomed in the background. I understood that both the patrons and employees must be wishing me away for their protection. I had to evacuate this cauldron, protect their lives and save myself by getting into the open! I laid down a generous amount to pay for the meal and a gratuity that would signify my regret at having involved them in undue danger. Rushing out I heard a popping sound as though from a small handgun. Moments later I could hear the siren of an ambulance. A voice arose saying that 'they' had killed your brothers. My entire body began to writhe and I moved a hand to my mouth to smother a scream of horror. I threw down my belongings with revulsion and raced up the street muttering Jesus, no! Pricking up my ears like an animal I sought to listen for the location of the ambulance, but I could no longer hear it. Instead what I heard was the sounding of clapping as gunfire in a civil war. There was bloody battle raging in the streets. I began to run the other way in convulsive shock like a mouse that has been bitten by a rattlesnake. Back and forth, back and forth, I ran. Then down to a gulley skirting the highway, I rushed. I tell you, I couldn't see straight! Suddenly everything subsided and I could hear laughter coming from afar. So this was nothing more than a hoax, I cried. I straggled back to the restaurant. My belongings were there where I had abandoned them. And there I sat awaiting the adoption by any tender heart and soft-spoken counsel. The snorting sounds of semi-trucks changing gears as they lurched ominously up and down the road assailed me. This devil's juncture seemed like a no-man's-land and reminded me dismally of the test ranges one finds in the desert. I smoked one cigarette after another trying to calm down after this dreadful experience. Yet I wondered if it ever took place. It was growing dark. There was a battered motel across the way but I couldn't bear the thought of sitting within the seedy hull of its walls. Others, no doubt, lay in wait to torture me with subliminal weaponry. I reentered the café trying to look composed and sat myself at the counter. When the waitress arrived I ordered coffee sensing a long night to come. I couldn't very well advertise myself as a vagrant and hence I proceeded to explain that I had disembarked at the wrong bus stop. I told her that I would have to bide my time here and continue south tomorrow. She didn't seem upset. In fact, she accepted it as though it was commonplace. This didn't surprise me so much as the indifference to my struggle that these people feigned. On full alert I sipped at my coffee pretending to be absorbed in my newspaper. After some time of performing this vigil I grew wary of certain grand interludes of silence. Every sound was as discrete as it was subtle, crisping like leather into my ears. I began to feel as though I was under a local anesthetic. I figured, faithfully, that it was the workings of the P.P.A. slipping something into my coffee. I could hear this queer plying and pulling as if a tumor was being excised from my flesh. It was, you see, as if my brain was attached to pedicles reaching into my heart and tied to the hindbrain. It reminded me of pulling a wetsuit over one's head while wearing earplugs. Within this numbing of the senses you could intuit the screams beneath the surface of things; hear the blowing wind, and the whip and crack of the arterial pulse. All glassy reflections from the windows were razor sharp and they began to rattle simultaneously like a deaf person's teacup and saucer. Stunned, I looked around. I felt as if I was seated at my own private movie, ensconced in this glass bubble. In my exhaustion I shortly nodded off for a brief nap. It was from within this chrysalis of sleep that I was visited with revelation. And I now fully realized the chilling horror of what was happening to me. 'They' were reading my mind through the vibrations of my larynx. By forcing me to mutter to myself they were performing the must invasive act possible – mind reading, sono-laryngeal-psycho-surveillance, or as I was to refer to it, SLPS! Good lord, my mind mirrored in waves of sound, I thought, and I came crashing back to reality with the consequence of this nightmare. As though inured to all suffering; my heart was replaced by a pendulum, my ears by a gramophone, my eyes by inhuman penetration, and now my voice, the ventriloquist's dummy. I lay in a stupor trying my best at efforts of sabotage. Eventually tiring in the slack of inattention, my mind would stubbornly roll and expose itself. I would redouble my efforts until I had, once more, become exhausted with pretext, and the syndrome would repeat itself. I took a walk and thought to myself, the war was lost, my enemy can read myheart at will, can manipulate me through the vulgarity of their expression. I am finished, through, dead from their implacable interrogations. All of my friends and family most likely subject to the same hapless fate. I scribbled in the dust, 'I surrender, SLPS.' Not knowing if this would have any effect upon my captors I said farewell on this most terrible of all nights. Finally, suffering from both shock and irresolution, I lumbered to my feet raving all the while to sabotage my thoughts. I still had to suckle the sleeve pressed to my mouth to wean away the horror. Having spent an eternity waiting for the bus morning light's blossom finally beckoned to me. I straggled down the road to meet the bus. Sitting as astute as a nervous desert rat for a few cool hours it finally arrived, gasping and coughing. With increasing traffic we entered the metropolitan area where it was necessary to transfer to another bus. The smoke of the city lay upon the horizon in thick tones of unpolished pewter. Everywhere the carbons and metals rose into gray and putty-brown clouds, closing around us like a steel cell. Occasionally flashes of copper gleamed with hypnotic scintillations, as though a chemical fire had ignited spontaneously. All spirit of place had vanished and the people that walked about appeared to be no more than bedraggled birds. The bus driver seemed to grow more agitated and alternately winced and grimaced at the sprawling convoy surrounding us. No doubt the uncontrollable dangers multiplied from within this lost municipality.

However, knowing that I was not far from my destination, surrendered to the rest of the trip steeped in memories of my past life. Time went by gracefully enough as I pleasantly teased myself with the happy anticipation of visiting the sky-wide ocean.

Part Three

I

The light trembled as if there had been arecent storm. The shoreline appeared ravaged from the thrashing waters, and the salt lay upon the swaying trees like frost. Haggard in the cool mirror of this aftermath the town's blanched buildings glimmered in the webs of light. The headlands looked like the columns of antiquity ready to be swallowed by the next great maw of the sea. The sun burned into my forehead and the seagulls tacked through the air like a boat jibing , then raising it's spinnaker to run with the wind. At the edge of the world I breathed deeply the drama of the sea burrowing into my brow. I was home! I walked along the deserted beach. The heavens seemed to recede, stealing fast into the horizon. The waves combed out their white curls invigorating communications. I scrawled into the sand another entry of my diary in the air, 'all action is prayer 'round the midnight sun.' Then I quickly effaced it. Remembrances soared of bathing in the sea, only returning home to cook out and share a bottle of wine with my friends and their happy smiles. My interrogations began. What friends? Where do they live? They prodded. I reflexively muttered in thought and speech, Salem; Jim, Santa Fe; Joyce, Chicago; Max, and on and on.... My object was to mask as well as possible the true identities with fiction. I continued on with these sonic titillations, babbling from the seamark to the city streets. The further that I distanced myself the more comfortable I became. Again, it was as though I was escaping from their range of frequency. As I was acquainting myself with the invisible nature of this beast I happened upon a government soup kitchen. Like so many other places of business, it looked as though it was set up with some haste. The menu was dirt cheap and the P.P.A. clientele was, once again, in good form.

Parading around in their aged vehicles they all, without exception, sported baseball hats. It looked like a scrap book from the great depression. Evidently they were aware of my diminishing funds and had chosen to prolong the pursuit with this generous dispensation of inexpensive meals. For what reasons, I confess, I did not know.Why, I felt very strongly, at one time, that their plan was to disguise and relocate me. However, with my latest discovery of 'their' evil instruments at work I now wagered that we were at a standoff, an impasse beyond which we could not go. The malicious form of a medium I had once used for the good of mankind was presently no more than my deathtrap. It's aberrant usage as either an instrument of surveillance, communications, or for the destruction of my internal organs persisted without pause. Oh, well, I sighed, pleased with the ease with which I was facing my sacrifices and hardships. Reduced to the elemental simplicity of food and shelter, to the primordial equation of survival I became aware of the tenacious wisdom of the spirit.

Yes, I was warming to the situation, pulling myself up by my own bootstraps, having a tender moment with myself. Life is simple and good, I thought, even though evil surrounds us. Let's toss this boomerang back and forth until death do us part and, what's more, have a good time of it despite the end. My thoughts were interrupted by one of these agents coughing. 'That's a fine how-do-you-do,' I muttered, stifling a laugh and forcing a cough myself. But my affection was short-lived. I had finished my meal and was polishing off my coffee when this maddened character made his entrance, playing the schizophrenic. Will there be no end to this jousting? I meditated. No doubt, a scathing commentary upon my psychiatrist's sickly portrait of me. My interest was piqued by this character who now sat next to me. How far, after all, could he take this? 'May I buy you a cup of coffee,' I offered, as if I hadn't noticed this form of intimidation. 'Yes,' he muttered abruptly as if I'd struck a nerve. Excusing his pretensions in order to conduct my own slippery inquiries, I sat untouched by his behavior. Why not repay him in kind and garnish the yield of patience, I collaborated with myself. His hair stood on end and he looked preternaturally alive. He continued on with gibberish. Let me tell you, he made absolutely no sense. I was never fond of exaggerated acting and silently reprimanded his performance as too utterly affected. He'll get caught at this game if he isn't more careful, I concluded. He rambled on not waiting for my reply. Believe me, he didn't want to be called down on his little bit of mischief-making as any actor doesn't wish to be slighted for his performance. As a result I merely gave him one of my see-through smiles. Why, I'd played this game before. It was as if a close friend was spinning a yarn. As always, since this game began, I would do best by taking a wait and see attitude, I counseled. Let him play his cards. How did he fit in? I wondered. From not only the indifference of these people toward him but their flagrant disregard verging on abuse I gathered he was from this evil other. Mimicking my past indiscretions for having visited a psychiatrist, I surmised. What a dupe and second rate actor. I felt some rage over his caricature of me after all that I had endured. At least I was now familiar with the lengths that they would venture to see my demise. Leave it alone, I consulted with myself, and don't show him the slightest visible trace of your suffering. As such I bade him farewell and, with a lilt to my stride, whistled a merry tune as I exited this government lean-to. It was one week since I had arrived at the coast. I discovered from consulting with the hotel clerk that this was the day of the solar eclipse. Would I see my desert friend from the P.P.A. or had he long ago vanished behind stage wings? Was this my day of reckoning? Was I to be extirpated from evil or hurled into the bloody horizon?

Was I to be extinguished in the smoking pyres of these sirens or resurrected upon a newborn wind, one no longer governed by this cheap and vibrant armature of manmade sound. I dragged myself to the beach as though I was headed to a funeral. A teeming crowd of people filled the shore, readying their specially prepared sunglasses to view the obstruction of the sun with superstitious expectancy. Cameras and video equipment were everywhere. This made me jumpy, to say the least. They all, at one time or another, seemed to be angling their sights in my direction. Again, 'they' must have been watching for any threats or indiscretions made toward me. I strolled leisurely to the green seamark, by a small promontory, in a bewitched daze. Having searched for so long to date, in vain, for the earmarks of a plan, any plan, my patience was thinning. Well, it was finally beginning to dawn on my weakened mind that if it had ever existed it was now lost among the chaparral, the desert, the mountains, the valleys, or the seashores I had roamed. Even these two separate entities, it seemed, were worn out with my rambling adventures. Or was this their plan to begin with, I reflected. Were they merely watching and waiting, losing all interest with my attrition, as I became less than the shadow of a man. Now I was near penniless, reduced to a pack and bedroll. How long, dear lord, had this series of events lasted. If I was a Robinson would I not notch out a calendar. However, I was no more than a lonely Friday, incapable of the articulation of one day to another. No, I was no longer able to calibrate life's meaning in my seething brain. My mind felt frail and restless, confused but prolific. It raced like a greyhound with nameless fear and excitability. The chorus at my back seemed to rise in pitch, dotting my mind with computer-like brail. I pointed my finger and slashed into the sand my little declaration, another passage for my secret diary. I was reaching to understand this wailing wall of noise. 'On this day, let it be known, that I, a man crowned by estrangement, delirious with the suffering of the quaternary; water, fire, earth, and my gnome-child, wind, metthis breach with the sacred on the misty shore, with a straw choir to his back. And I could walk no more.' Soon I brushed out this plea frightened by the attentions of the SLPS. Sitting motionless and assailed with others speech, I succumbed to the sighing rhythm of the white magnificence scrubbing the rocks at my feet. I brushed my wounded temples with this salty poultice of the earth and rinsed my infested ears. And as I occasionally glanced at this shade being drawn I became spellbound by this turning waterwheel. The breath of each tide, each vital pulse, as sacred as a family quietly sleeping. Above me a broken sundial invoked the birds premature cries of dusk. Now the waters gaped at me struggling in the sun-darkened anguish. And there, I wept uncontrollably. I bowed my head, a lost, bereaved child from a civilization that no longer existed, that would never exist for me again! I slowly composed myself, not really so embarrassed by this unrestrained sobbing. There behind me lay a thousand souls bathed in this violet dusk. Church bells rang out and I wondered if there was any consoling message within this fugue. But I had nobody now, and it was quite impossible in my nervous state, to summon the words for any communion owever small. The city streets were deserted and I had, I realized, missed the finishing touches to this natural spectacle - a swim! I strode back to the beach intent upon waking myself up with a good chill. I savagely made my way past the breaking water. Whether it was due to my weakened condition I wasn't sure but the slivers of cold ice cut into me and the ocean seemed to ruthlessly churn, almost angry at the sun's disappearance. Great ropes of water unfurled their noose around me. I usually enjoyed swimming but now I was fighting from drowning in this vast power. Fortunately I was soon safely beyond the current and I found myself rejoicing in my newborn vigil.

The next day I counted what money remained. Enough, I realized, to last me two more nights of this restless motel life. Then it would be up to providence. Who knows, I thought, if I could become a little more street wise with time! But the grotesque absurdity of this chase, poisoning, and surveillance was boring into me more and more. I had been robbed not only of every pleasure but of sustenance as well. Spend the remaining money as if it was your last day on earth, my friend, I heard myself rally to my satisfaction. Why, buy a delicious meal and take in a good show, you deserve it, I continued. I felt somewhat resuscitated by this line of reasoning. Of course, you pagan sensualist, enjoy your senses beyond this wind tunnel. Bury this evil in the wake of your ecstasy! But moments later the needles and pins of my fear began to prick at me and I slowly began to lose some of my former bravado. I was strolling downtown when a man exiting an Italian restaurant suddenly coughed. Well, if you can't beat them, join them, I reconciled, and coughed loudly once. Perhaps, I'll bid the don best wishes with a sly wink. But my stomach must have shrunk for soon I felt sated to the point of nausea. To add to this I was being scrutinized and glowered at by staff and patrons alike. Even if they were envious of my bravery had they forgotten mutual respect altogether. I spied a local theater showing the latest film. It would seem from the advertisement upon the window that it was a dip into madness played by a well-known comedian. I paid admission and sauntered into the black pitch of the theater. Having some difficulty in the darkness I finally found a seat. Though I couldn't clearly make out expressions nor conversations I could easily sense the same curiosity about me that had been following me in the streets. I enjoyed this secret life of the darkness as the audience was, from time to time, blinked by the light from the film. I watched the central character feigning a repertoire of visual hallucinations unable to conceive of such a form of lunacy. Consequently I began to lose interest in this contrived phantasmagoria. Was that what it was like to be taken by madness, I wondered. Then the movie fell back to earth and became more true to life, more suitable to my taste. Our madman of stage and screen now reached for something upon the ground. He was with a woman of his fancy before sharing a meal. He took this piece of wire which lay upon the ground and artfully fashioned it into a present for his beloved. Suddenly I could take no more. Tears began to flood down my cheeks at this moment of tenderness. I wiped off my face with my sweater and aborted the movie before its conclusion. I made my way out down the aisle with the help of little lamps, like fallen stars.The air felt refreshing but I was still silently hiccoughing with tears from deep within. I sped up one street, then two, always keeping my head down, tired of this game of pursuit. I continued at a jogging pace made a right turn, then after a few more blocks I turned left. Finally I approached a bridge. I began to cross but suddenly stopped, like a deer struck by the hypnotic trails of light. Waves of sloping vibration seemed to edge in upon me. As if this grand inquisitor was focusing on me in my stillness, I looked down at the traffic. It scrambled into a darkness that now resembled the theater. The cars headlights flashed their fleeting beams of light around me like the screen's silver light upon the audience. A voice issued from some grave hinterland, 'go ahead, jump' it coaxed. My imagination grew vivid with this suggestion. Down a frontage road I saw a parked police car as though danger was imminent. My legs began to buckle and tremble to the vibrations of the bridge and the chorus around me. I fell down unable to stand any longer. I feared being brushed over the railing like a leaf. My heart sank and, after groveling like a beggar upon this rocking parapet, I hugged onto the trunk of a tree. I was, at last, safe!

A few days later I walked out from the shadows of my motel feeling as though I was, once again, escaping from my captors. My room had become filled with velvet-tongued flirtations from some well-hidden succubus and a maelstrom of incantations and secret biddings broke up my sleep. The few paper dollars I found looked like foreign script. My pocket change shone jewel bright. The sky hung high over head as soft as a baby's blanket. The world felt full of promise as I drew closer to this primacy of freedom I had never known. As if the well-meaning stranger in some ancient myth I sauntered down the road, all worldly goods fastened to my back. As I walked in the gentle sunlight, stripped of all purpose, my soul became as naked as the sky, and my mind grew more and more listless. It was autumn, my favorite season. In the purity of this soft flame, under the high, longing fall air, the trees glittered bereft of the cloying heat of summer. They lolled like dolls from side to side, swaying as a newborn unsteadily moves his head. The flowers, like shades of lipstick, were as pleasing as the lips of a woman. This wooing of light mixed with a fine moisture brushed every surface. It conspired to make of this pristine world a place conceived happily, lovingly. I drank from the air swilling the fragrant coolness, the will of my tongue burning in the fire of the few deciduous leaves that lay upon the ground. After walking for some time, cast within the day's spell, I awoke to realize that I was on the coastal road far from town. In the distance I gazed at the ruffled veils of water slowly advancing, tilting and bobbing, in the frail-colored light. My merry mood and divine confidence had carried me long and far from the city where I had born witness to the solar eclipse and partaken of more than one bitter-tasting experience. I sat by the roadside a little perplexed at my situation and tossed a coin in the air to decide my direction. Out of habit I looked at my wrist to find the time and date but realized I had pawned it some time ago. Perhaps it might be a good idea to draft a calendar so that I might not lose sight of time altogether. I thought. However, not knowing the date I abandoned this plan for the moment, and briefly recalled the calendar of my desert friend. Sitting thus, resting my legs, I stuck out my thumb. Before I knew it a truck pulled over. I hopped in, head down, wondering if I was throwing this poor boy's life to the wolves. But he was so carefree and full of life that I suddenly forgot my situation. In fact, he reminded me of myself, owning the world with his youth, as I had once done. He told me of his destination. It was a town with which I was familiar that lay inland a few miles. I quickly exclaimed 'just my luck, that's where I am going!' Though I was a little surprised at this decision I remembered that it was a quaint sort of place, given up to individual businesses and shop merchants. It was near a park, too, where I might take a bird bath now and then. This young man, no doubt from the Public Protection

Agency, courageously offered me a few dollars. However, I told him that my haggard appearance was no more than the result of research for my new book. I was, in fact, very well off, I continued, resurrecting myself in his eyes from my untidy state of affairs. I could tell that he respected this tiny bit of make-believe as his eyes seemed to grow watery. He dropped me off and I rejoiced from within. 'Hallelujah!' I shouted inwardly. My brothers and sisters rapt, as we were, in this curious drama shuffled everywhere about me. Not a look out of place, mind you, not one! The genuflections from my loving companions as good as a nod and a wink. All of these smiling eyes glittering in the thin, chilled air. It brightly appeared to be no more nor less than an intimate travesty. But for one brief moment, I thought to myself, perhaps the young man in the car was my nephew in disguise. My, what eminent playwright could duplicate such perfection; such quick, liquid, and unswerving motion forward. 'The pulse of the city' they say! Well, this is certainly the play of all plays to crown that glory. Each of us moving like blood from the heart. 'Hallelujah,' I cried. They had, already, set up my security with the utmost fastidiousness. Some cars chased while others seemed to be pushed to the side. I began to wonder if the cars were not somehow driving themselves so determined and thoughtless had they become. A blanket of agents strode in and out of the shops, harbingers of my arrival. No doubt, they were busy propagating the subtle language of their communication, laying safety nets for another one of my high wire routines through danger and oblivion. I was so familiar with their modus operandi, I had to laugh. The well versed could indisputably perceive that he environs, likewise, had become informed by this waving peristalsis of communication. Why you couldn't wander down an alley, a park, the ocean, or a mountain trail without being espied from somewhere. Invariably a car alarm, a cough, or a horn would sound at my approach. Without exception a flag or baseball cap would appear. But I must ask, isn't the human face the most remarkable and memorable of anyone's experience? After all, its diversity and features are unfathomable. It's so fantastically heroic and complex, so simple and divine, or so overwhelmed, and troubled. And in the end so forgiving and forgivable. But what is this mean-spiritedness that looms in the air? No matter, each and everyone of us is singled out to bear the burden of our short fables. Just watch the lone patron eating by themselves, their sad courage dreaming patiently. Surely, one day we must be reunited in a more human kinship. I shuffled about town smiling to myself over the grandiose stakeout being laid. Everyone slipping into their costumes, taking their proper places and assuming their own distinctive postures. There was an abundance of cafes and different cuisine and one or two bookstores lined every street. My stomach was gnawing at me and fantasies of food were making me ravenous with hunger. I took out my bottle of water and drank greedily from it. This seemed to cut through my appetite as it had so many times before. The door to a restaurant stood open and a crowd of noisy patrons either booed or applauded a game being broadcast. Two large television set mounted upon each corner wall blared out their event as if it happened but once in a lifetime. I noticed some hotplates on a dining table and realized that hors d'oeuvres were being served. Walking in nonchalantly, I headed for the restroom. After relieving myself I slipped over to the service table and quickly and deftly stuffed my pockets with carrots, celery, and cold cuts of meat. Fortunately nobody seemed to notice me. The customers were watching the games and the employees busy at work, I supposed, though I didn't really believe it for one second. I departed as silently as I had entered. If, after all, the P.P.A. was going to ignore me so wasn't this 'take all you like' attitude their message? It was dusk and the sun was falling into the sea. The most relaxing time of the day had arrived. I came upon a church and sat at its steps to dole out my ration of food for the night. Suddenly, I began hearing the plaintive cooing of a dove. But that wasn't all. Mingling fantastically into its tone so that it would go unnoticed by the unobservant passer-by, was my dear sister's voice. 'I-feel-so-sorry-for-you,' it strangely cooed. I looked down at a crack in the pavement munching on a carrot stick, feeling very sad. My temples felt numb and my eyes were droopy. Then in soft, soothing whispers there came a strangers voice, 'we're giving you your medicine now,' it crooned. So that was it, I realized, why there was no notice given me, no fuss made over my taking these few simple items. I lay back surrendering to this hypnotism, any trace of vibrancy from this energetic day disappearing. I slid into a cool and not altogether unpleasant melancholy as the ministrations of the dove continued. And I began to wonder about their peaceful habitus understanding why 'they' were using the dove to conceal my sister's voice. Such a message was certainly in her nature, and I applauded the P.P.A. for its compassion. In this vacant lull I sat propped up with my chin in my hand ready to surrender, even if it be to death. Like a calf at the slaughterhouse I simply rolled my eyes in a stupor. Meanwhile the dove kept up this doleful message while I grew more numb, more subordinate to a fate which lay outside of my will. The medication seemed to soften the cold, bruising ache of my isolation.

After an hour of this gravesite mourning on the stoop of an abandoned, medieval-looking church, I walked by its slim sidewalk to a small garden grown wild with neglect. I found myself a bush to crawl into and lay like an animal in its lair. A cat was not far off, doing a little nocturnal hunting. As he sat there I carefully watched his ears to alert me to any approaching danger. Soon thereafter, medicated and with thoughts of nothing in particular, I drifted off to sleep. Awaking to a glorious, cool morning, I packed my worldly remains upon my back and reentered the ragged, diminutive town. I came upon a coffee house and ducked inside. Refills were free and there was plenty of iced water as well. I sat beneath a tree and took out a frayed book of poems from my knapsack. Shortly thereafter I began to silently fill the air with readings for the troops, as it were. The young waitress, frisky and full of light, wandered over. She remarked of her admiration for the poet's work, then proceeded to share her favorite poem with me. Yes, that's so beautiful I sighed, thinking more of her beauty than that of her words. We continued to share in mutual confidence as best we could from within this vast hallway of audible mirrors reflecting my thoughts aloud. With her soft complexion she looked as though she had just stepped from out of a painting. Beneath the striped awnings of the café shadows fell like masks, dappling the thick lips of voluptuaries blowing their plumes of blue smoke. The timid, the bold, the resigned, the criminal all sipping from cups together upon the tarmac arrested my attention. The roses of the cheeks of young women, the light gleaming from the robust, and the laughter spilling out into the street overwhelmed me and took me by surprise. But finally, fearing everyone's safety and honoring the waitresse's attentiveness I moved on. Besides it was becoming more difficult to focus on a poem with the drone of communications constantly at my back. Oh, how I sickened of this 'audio-colossus!' I paraded up and down the tree-flanked boulevards bidding people 'good morning' into the air. The eternal shopkeepers were busy sweeping and watering down their sidewalks in preparation for another day of business, seemingly oblivious of my great misfortune of injury. Having grown conspicuous after practicing these exercises I walked south and away from the center of this wheel. I passed through a few older neighborhoods until the park shone in full view. There people jogged or lounged in idleness, whiling away the hours. Some of them were as placid as the trees that stood like guardians upon the green ground. Shopping carts full of bric-a-brac dotted the park. Mostly made up in ragged fashion now or spouting out gibberish so as to appear the wreckage of humanity, the P.P.A. reclined in folds. Harassed by the SLPS sensors I needed to be alone and I walked to a knoll's edge by a cluster of eucalyptus. If you stared long enough you could finally distinguish the heavy flow of traffic beyond the cool ravine. This unnerving noise seemed to gather into currents and then concuss about me. I sat down, hemmed in, not knowing where to retreat. After growing more anxious I shambled back toward town. On my return a small child waved from a passing car and this seemed to halve the weight upon my shoulders. But as I entered the town an old woman sat hunched by a tin for donations. What range and fortitude these good people possess, I puzzled, and began to wonder what mission she was fulfilling. As though she was about to expire upon these city plains her eyes vaguely flickered in their sockets. I walked over to her and put a few coins into her cup hoping that I wasn't endangering her with this gesture. Such a sad bundle of rickety bones draped in rags. Her unforgettable death mask hung upon her breast in defeat, like the head of a dead bird. Was this what the struggle to venerable old age was about in this land.

No, undoubtedly, she wore the untiring expression of the P.P.A. How else could one explain this offering, of the old to the dust, like a forgotten article in a rummage sale? Later that evening I stationed myself at the entrance to the restaurant where I had the night before snuck away with a free dinner. After a long spell of waiting, like a cat for a saucer of milk, I realized that there were no snacks being laid out. Evidently that was only on Mondays. I would have to remember the days of the week and all of the various establishments for obtaining free provender. In my confusion and with such a bad case of nerves it seemed impossible for me to summon the tenacity for procuring bottles and cans. No, I would have to follow a more facile approach to solve my dilemma of thirst and hunger. Fluids were no problem as I could always fill my water bottle at the hospital or park. Disappointed and hungry I walked amidst the heart of the city. Up an alleyway

I scrambled trying to stay clear of traffic patrolling the streets where porch lights burned like cressets. More signs of the P.P.A. on alert, I thought. These timeless alleyways seemed to beckon like a finger and provided the consolation of sweet memory. But some lanky kid with a chip on his shoulder passed by uttering 'get a job.' The sudden blows of crime lingered darkly in his eyes. I returned to him his own pernicious look and responded, 'gladly, give me a job.' However, he kept on walking and muttering incorrigibly 'get a job.' A nitwit and proud of it, eh! No doubt one of the dirty hands of evil, I concluded, glad to be done with it.I found a nook behind a business. As it was deserted I made myself at home. I fell upon my bedroll and began to think about the alleyway where my grandmother, my sister, and I used to walk hand in hand to the neighborhood's grocery store. There we would buy ice cream before an afternoon's dreamy nap. All of us bathing in the divine silence that is true peace of mind and soul. We would glide through the day filled with volumes of untold love, as timeless and sure of our natural course as nature. I leaned back humming pleasantly like my grandmother used to do, and lay steeped in this refuge of memory. I was free, for the moment, from the roaming of men and beasts. About one week passed by. I couldn't be sure. The trail of gasping echoes still plunged slowly from nearby dwellings, or would pelt down like shrapnel around me. At other times things began to soften, so much, in fact, that I thought every source of despair had vanished. But it would return with a vengeance. I continued to adapt as best I could playing leisurely games, parlaying with these miscreants, insulting them, then giving them the boot with the rhetoric of reprisal. Yes, I would rally, make a football out of this ring-down and drive it through the field posts.

And I would fire chivalrously into the

sky with their broadcast, muttering, Quixote is slaying our windmill!' Again and again, in triumphant victory, I rubbed the noses of these looters and sackers into their own excrement.

Meanwhile the neighborhoods and the township itself were becoming as familiar as if I had grown up here. It was as though I was in a state of childhood at times. I would seek out and explore the same wonders and little mysteries of the world with dream and fantasy at my back. At other times, as I say, all hell broke loose until I thought I might succumb to my convulsions. Thank the powers that be for my medication, for like some apothecary of nature, it kept these parasites at bay.

II

The dawn came with its divine rhythm and colors. The sky opened like a seashell, all rose and nacre, like it was the first morning of the universe. Feeling the need for a warm drink I scampered passed the many cafes determined to drink the remnants left by people that had been in a hurry. I finally found one and drank it down in one gulp, then I vanished like an apparition. But I began to curse the P.P.A. for their miserly selves. After all, what fear could this netherworld pose that a man could no longer enjoy a cup of coffee?

As usual my next stop was the hospital. It was always the most convenient location to take my ablutions. If they interceded in such basic needs I would blow the roof off with them. For these devils were beginning to make more sense than goodness. No, I would tell them all 'how the cow ate the cabbage.' Why mince words in struggling times such as these? I began to have no compassion for their lame idiocy. Why not flush all of our pretenses straight down to hell? But I realized that the entire world was balking. I had been through every social hallway by now, of justice, law, and medicine.

The day passed much like any other as I restlessly paced to and fro through town, mumbling at war with these voices. When I was forced to speak more than a few words I would began to stutter. It was as though I was continually being interrupted by allies and enemies alike. I began to miss, more and more, singularity of mind. My lot, it seemed, was to diet with this steady confusion, these underlings popping up like so many soap bubbles. Bizarre spontaneities and insights erupted with great speed and confusion, each time ringing a little more loudly.

As nervous as a bird I bent to pick up cigarette ends like a pigeon pecking at crumbs in the park. Suddenly the horrendous noise of a leaf blower struck me down. These engines were as crazy as a mockingbird. What other clever ruse will this evil have up their sleeves for me, I questioned angrily. But I could no longer follow my thoughts. Addled by such traps set by my nemesis I was forced, once more, to move on.

I walked as fast as my legs would take me, chattering to myself with a wild superabundance of energy. A voice rose, presumably from the P.P.A. warning once again, 'they're killing you with ultrasound.'

I could feel my insides warming and my stomach felt as though it was being squeezed by hot tongs. I sat down upon the curb holding onto myself, gritting my teeth, gasping for air, as my throat reverberated to this hostile assault. "Ugh I cried, shaking to the core.

After some time the affects began to

wear off but a bus pulled over and a few of its passengers disembarked. One of them, an old man with long, yellow locks and a silver, flowing beard, screamed at the top of his lungs, cursed the sky, and shook his fist menacingly in the air. Was this act meant for me alone, I mused. Was this what 'they' had in store for me, I quaked inwardly. Am I to become no more than a walking malapropism for others entertainment? Am I to become a modern, demented jester of this new world court?I traversed the all too familiar streets back to the park. The grass had just been freshly cut and I lay back convalescing from the intrusions of the day, smelling the sun-baked lawns. All about me people walked as dutifully as automata. Their averted eyes or blank stares were almost insufferable.

Where was I to go to escape this pervasive lunacy and my relentless pursuit? How was I to win my freedom? But my appetite came soaring back, leaving me with a dull, visceral ache.I picked myself up and marched back toward the city measuring my stride to the bruising and throbbing of my hunger. The earth seemed to sway and the dwellings reminded me of a cozy harbor, filled with barges and houseboats. I entered a market to be near my fantasy of food and to smell the vegetables and fruit. All around me peaceful foot soldiers formed the unrequited love and unbroken circle of their curious affections. In the quiet lengths of damp air 'they strolled silently and patiently through the aisles. Within my brain I was swapping stories for the sake of tradition, having another fine moment with myself.

Meanwhile, above me within the old ceiling fan the voice emanating from the dove's song. Only this time, rather than lament, it giggled and danced with a thrilling flush. "Take anything you like, these little girls tittered. "Yeah, that's right" the other chimed in. I pocketed a small baguette, then a bar of cheese, and walked out not caring about traditional customs of payment. No, I belonged to another more simple code of ethics, and I glided down the aisle with the impunity of a foreign diplomat. I continued to walk, scurrying down an alleyway, excited by the prospects of consuming this delicious meal. One alley after another I tramped, impatient to get to the park, feeling light and mischievous, cooing to myself. I found a clearing in a grove of eucalyptus. There I sat to eat my sandwich washing it down from time to time with water. I lit a cigarette butt and reclined in the darkness noticing the appearance of a small bracelet of stars. Life was good again! I espied a tarp down below where presumably the P.P.A. was a tarp stationed. I lay down with resignation and shortly nodded off. When I awoke it was in the midst of the night. A hundred oddities seemed to buzz into my ears from the thicket of darkness, or alighted upon rooftops of the neighboring building. Looking up into the frostbitten sky, the stars seemed to be glimmering from a brush of great magnetic waves. I lay there without a wish and drifted softly back to sleep. A city bus awoke me. With a tremendous clatter it forged ahead, leaving a thick trail of black smoke. 'First things first' I told myself, and began to organize my agenda while tying up my baggage. As it was still early only a few troops knocked about, a few stragglers and sleepy heads.

Grateful for their thoughtful protection I smiled softly and headed for my constitutional birdbath at the hospital. Why, there was no telling how much quiet adulation lay beneath this theatrical calm. Perhaps, after this situation was remedied we might all meet in an embrace of shared love, as confused victors of battle. Hadn't a young man, without the slightest fear for his own life, slipped me two dollars only a few nights before as I rested with one eye open. No, there was nothing so precious as an act of human kindness. Even though these gestures seemed to diminish with age, they still sent the arrow of love to one's heart.

A mean-spirited chorus arose taunting me, 'make tracks, you hunchback, make tracks!' Feeling a beaten fool in this shadow play I began to mope along, matching my posture to the curvature of my mental state. I walked down the busy thoroughfare hunched up, dragging one leg, feeling exiled and succumbing to the voices whim.

The mean fascist symbols of some criminal lined a wall. Below it, presumably one of the P.P.A., had written 'God save this town.' I shook my head feeling sad for bringing trouble to these people. But what was I to do? These same hieroglyphics of murder lay everywhere I went! Out of the corner of my eye I caught sight of a policeman. A painful look seemed to cross his face, as if to say, 'we're doing all we can, yet isn't it a shame.' I began to awaken from my cowardice. 'No need to collapse into a state of hopeless defeat,' I counseled, 'they're doing everything they can.'Leaning upon a garden wall I fell into a melancholy mood. Two quotations that I had once read suddenly sprang into my mind. I decided to enter them in the annals of my diary. I swiftly traced into the air with my finger their content."God is nature without man,"(~ *Honore de Balzac*) and then a more soothing sentiment, "All my idols have feet of clay." *(~Albert Camus)* Somehow I felt as if this was the perfect equation being worked out day by day. 'From within this topsy-turvy world I was finding my lodestar!' I exclaimed.

Come hell or high water I would adapt and sidle by this world giving it a good nudge. I would bear the signature of my trials in this audio-colossus, I thought, gurgling to myself.

Walking down the street, erect with my new spirits, I realized thing were not that bad. If the police were to drive by I would not let on to our form of complicity.

Perhaps, emboldened by my new equation, I would begin to take things in stride, illustrating my cooperative character and the good-natured person I had once been. Yes, I would make a subtle sign. By scratching my brow, I might give some indication of my appreciation for their good work. For no matter what of this plague was to persist and be endured did I not still owe these good people my life for their perseverance? The day passed as I trembled and burned with introspection. All around me cars cut smartly through space. Motion played against motion. For instance, the man raising a hand to his head could set off a traffic light, crossing a pedestrian, who by disturbing a puddle, would inspire a breeze. That breeze would, in turn, drop a leaf and waft against the shiny pinwheel of the toddler, whose carriage careened down grinding columns of light. Meanwhile, shop windows reflected the crowd's frenetic gestures; stooping to tie a shoe, waving a cane, lighting a cigarette, crossing a street, to all begin, once again, in the amazing shuffle of light. The streets were a violent racetrack of gleaming cars, trucks, vans, and motorcycles raging to some well orchestrated, preordained flow of traffic. They merged and dispersed like atoms. Groaning and sputtering their entrails to the heavy-footed commands of their impatient owners, they skittered the road blindly. Everywhere horns honked, car alarms sounded, and people with baseball caps walked about. Even the cool air itself seemed to be a plenum of crystals yielding this beveled -mirror appearance. It was the same raging hustle that I had recognized so painfully long ago.

I retreated to the alcove of a children's train store that had just closed. I saw the owner hang the closing sign with a languishing sigh. Either his expression was founded upon a day of no sales or the P.P.A. had passed the word to him of my need for a place to rest. A little dazed I sat recuperating from another brush with the ultrasound. A young woman walked shyly toward me with a curious expression of wonder. She looked as though she was suffering from exposure or some wasting disease. Her skin was mottled by raw, pink pigment like scar tissue. I marveled again at the lengths toward which these two parties had committed themselves. It must have taken days to put on her makeup! However, her performance was at best nothing more than a cliché of mental illness. She seemed to grow friendly and then quite quickly would turn on her heels, only to return a few moments later to mutter to herself. She sat down and proceeded to roll me a cigarette with gnarled, stubby fingers. I applauded both her generosity and bravery. She seemed, beneath all appearances, to fear for her own wellbeing, well aware of the dangers of my situation. I could see through her disguise now and could almost imagine her engaged in training sessions at the bureau for performing this routine. She giggled self-consciously and I said nothing to give her away. I accepted her gift graciously and soon she was gone like the spectral, failing light.

However, in predictable fickleness, she arrived once more. She approached cautiously, as if wishing to be commended for her dramatics. Leaning down to peer down my shirt, apparently to satisfy her daft-like curiosity, she presently stepped back. What acting, I thought, prepared for such a pretext and I replied without meditation and in jest — 'have you ever played fiddle at the barn-raising dance?'

On cue, she giggled again, self-consciously, turning apple-red, and vanished into the night. Yeah, I thought with a cocky raised brow, I've done a little acting myself by now. I wasn't going to be shown who was who by any agency, any organization, no matter what their allegiance or origin might be.

In my stupor I pondered my fate. The

dazzling sunlight had come and gone, pulled like a thistle, and the night was pricked with stars. Numb I gazed with indifference at the traffic. Suddenly it dawned on me! Was it not important to be taken in officially? Was this not the only way to elude this evil, to grasp the nature of this peril through clear and definitive

Briefings?

I raced quickly toward the hospital intending to commit myself. Surely then they would be able to sequester me from this onslaught and prepare me for my new life. As I hastened across town the tempo of things began to pick up. It was as though the message of all messages had finally penetrated my stubborn, confused mind.

All about me people seemed to sense my object and direction as they led me toward destiny. Utterly convinced that I had reached the great watershed of my deliverance I glided to the emergency room. To be perfectly honest I felt like blubbering with joy! In the distance, the elasticity of vibrations struck high and low, like a French police siren.

I informed the receptionist of my condition, casting myself in a dangerous light, garbling my speech intentionally, and fidgeting through my pockets. The sad, patient eyes of others around me seemed to say, 'oh, but we're glad you've made it.' Some of them had probably been with me since the beginning and traveled the many endless miles of my journey. Dawdling away the time, I sat paging through multitudes of loveless phantoms and the debris of my expeditions. A finger pressed, like a local anesthetic, into my forehead. Medication was again being administered. Finally my name was called. My vital signs were taken along with a simple, fictitious history I had invented in the waiting room. I was given an injection, probably a placebo to fool these vicious demons, and left alone for twelve eternities.

My patience was running thin when an ambulance driver and his attendant rolled in their gurney. By all means, boys, let's make it look good, I suspired. I heard the driver whisper something about ultrasound. We arrived at the county mental hospital. I was wheeled in, then asked to wait for the doctor. It seemed again as though hours had passed before bureaucracy was satisfied. Perhaps the infinite details of my departure demanded a liberal amount of time. I could almost hear the engines of my private jet light up in some awaiting arena. I munched on a sack lunch they had given me and dreamed of faraway places.

Presently I met with an intake counselor, then was asked to wait again. By the time the doctor was prepared to see me some of my eagerness had disappeared.

Ambiguities began to assail me left and right. After being subjected to this mental magistrate's scrutiny I became confused. Were they not aware of my situation, these imperious clucks, or wasn't there a compassionate thought in their little minds?

I wondered.

The doctor came out to deliver the final blow. 'No, we cannot accept you,' he stated firmly. It was that simple to him. By now it was quite late. He handed me a bus token and said goodbye. I was stunned! I angrily stomped out. It felt good to be out of this cold, metal cage, painted and polished like a lavatory.

It was simple to me now. Trust nobody, no message, no thought, I concluded. I puffed on a cigarette end bracing myself for the same tedious world, teeming with surveillance. Feeling indignant toward their methods I cursed the doctor up and down. I felt like taking retribution against all of these so-called well-wishers of the P.P.A. and sped down the road chattering to myself.

I was used up. There was no point in my returning to town and the buses didn't seem to be running this time of night. I recalled a route to a nearby beach community. There, at least, I might be able to bathe at the public showers and sleep upon a soft bed of sand. Yes, I thought, I was through the city life. I would return to the blessed ocean. There I could wander without the problems of being landlocked.

No more would I be cordoned off by traffic, cement, and ominous graffiti, nor would I be badgered by drunks, skunks, and madmen.

III

The waters rumbled and undulated drowning the prints of sandpipers. Seabirds cried and grazed the air or stood nursing themselves on the beauty of the horizon. Salt mingled with the cool air engendering forgetfulness and ageless nostalgia. The perfumes of myth and dream for troubled souls filled the air. And there faintly in the distance lay my enemy gossiping and plotting in a polyphony of whispers.

The night walk here had exhausted me but I was finally able to land upon this bluff of sand in the pitch of night as providence would have it. Daylight had now all but put an end to blind imaginings and the unsettling rumors of darkness and I was pleased to see fewer people about me. At least the P.P.A. was beginning to respect my limits. A few morning walkers and a school of surfers that looked like seals dotted the sea. I felt lighter having returned from this dusty odyssey and looked forward to a cup of coffee. Using my hat to panhandle money from the street now busy with tourists I finally, after an hour, had enough for a cup of coffee. The P.P.A., why do I implore you so after all of these misgivings?

Why, I smirked, you have whittled me down to a scrawny stick, ground me into nothing more than coffee. Let them pay for their deeds, I bellowed. If this rapacious evil has overtaken them, I growled, it falls upon all of our hearts, all sense of justice!

Something inside insisted that nobody was making accusations and I felt some remorse at this muted outburst. Outside danger lay everywhere!

I massaged my temples at the corner of the main city street. Then I leaned upon a wall, expiring beneath the sun's brazen stare. Shops filled with bathing suits and beach ware alternated with restaurants grilling fish or selling plates of pasta. A shopkeeper from two doors down eyeballed me in a threatening way. Like an animal turning to pace his empty cage he reentered his shop. No more than a minute had passed by when he reappeared with the same ferocity in his eyes. His head was shaped like a bell, his eyes were narrow and his broad forehead prominent. In phrenology, he portrayed the dumb and violent. He grumbled, then spat upon the ground. With his arms akimbo, stalwart and mean, he demanded "leave, get out of here!" He now shook his head like an idiot, stewing in his own juices of anger. Saliva, like blood, seemed to ooze from the gash of his mouth. You fool, I thought,

I can't control what hardships have struck me down and the great distant miles you've put me through. And I began to think hard upon my many misfortunes as this adversarial climate soared around me. He merely stared at me and I thought about what an animal man was in the last resort. I tell you, though I was quaking in my boots, I was ready to bust out of this penitentiary into a storm of anger. Finally, he ducked back into his shop with irresolution while I sighed like the frightened animal he had made of me. I thought, you idiot, none of your institutions will have me yet you fume and quibble about a man leaning against a wall. Why had all understanding become replaced by this violent moral clamor? But soon I began to soften with remorse and, once again, moved on as always toward nowhere. Each day came and went shapelessly by, marked only by the motion of the heavens, as people flitted about to complete their assignments. The sun and its siblings of the moon and stars continued to light up the sky above this churning axle of the sea. But as comforting as it was the emptiness of myfugitive retirement remained.

Meanwhile, I walked tirelessly, drinking water to appease my appetite. I began to grow weary of these people and my surroundings. It was true that there was one market on my side. As the P.P.A. had entire control over it there was never a complaint when I pocketed a slender meal of fruit or nuts. However, my resources were limited by this scarcity of businesses and the criminal element seemed to be proliferating around me as well. Loud, threatening music boomed from the parking lots of the main beach where broken down cars sat with their low brow idlers. You could smell crime in the air stagnating under the garish neon lamps. As though a trail of orange vapors lighting the way for some Jack the Ripper they flickered among the silhouettes of rude, prowling young men. The lighting and cruel crowd reminded me of satanic worshippers arc welding in the midst of night. Only a very few older couples with dogs or young lovers on the alert braved the dark shore.

The P.P.A. was running thin! I walked out of town noting these odds changing against me. Away from the coast I fled from these reprobates and upstarts when I was suddenly struck by something. 'You've been shot,' my voices uttered in pain. I felt a hot sting and collapsed to the ground, my body in shock.

My respiration was in distress and it was difficult to draw a breath. My heart leapt from my chest and I blurted out, 'help!'

However people only stared at me with disgust. The buildings seemed to sway and the cars swam by me with distortion. My face was soaked in a cold sweat. I began to lose consciousness. Waves of fear viciously attacked my body. I naturally assumed this to be the final degradation of the body's performance. 'Better to die with simple joys than compete for ruins,' I surrendered.

But then I began to awaken from this siege. Something inside me told me to stand up, that it was alright. And I did so unsteadily realizing that this was just another stunning blow from the evil powers at work. I walked along now alone and proud, cursing both sides for their ineffectual selves. A police car pulled over.

Had they finally come for me? I wondered. But my expectations were tempered by the one solitary police car showing up among this colossal convoy.

'We've heard complaints of you shouting out loud at everybody,' he remarked solemnly. 'No,' I muttered sheepishly, looking out for his safety as these demons lurched by in their automobiles. 'Identification, sir,' he demanded. I rummaged through my gear and found my passport. While he ran it through his computer I sat upon the curb, dry-spitting with nausea. Finally he reappeared. After giving me a brief lecture and correcting my behavior, he climbed into his car and quickly sped off into the distance. The harbinger of moral injunctions in a world to which I no longer belonged. Goodness me, his hands are tied too. As if that should come as any surprise,

I thought. Trampled by every conceivable misfortune, and all of these fools wish only to proscribe, I exclaimed inwardly with dejection. I trundled back to the beach on the qui vive. Any morning hope I may have had for searching out a new day was already exhausted. Noticing a community gathering at a neighborhood house, I wandered in. I picked through some brochures. It was an A.A. meeting and the mood was somber. Nobody seemed to notice me or were privately distancing themselves for fear of the danger that loomed around us. I spied some coffee brewing. Nonchalantly I poured myself a paper cup and slowly slunk out of sight. I whistled and walked keeping my thoughts above the sordidness of this superhuman feat. Rhyming my pace to the companionship of my childhood, I crossed the street to enter a small library. It was pleasantly quiet except for the faint volley of whispers coming from one of these two ubiquitous factions. I could smell the musty jackets and it reminded me of a fruit orchard in late summer. I inhaled deeply expectant of a breathtaking reunion with my old friends who had, likewise, hustled through their own struggling lives. They, it seemed, had reached out to console the family of man with the miraculous fingerprints of the alphabet.

However, to my horror opening each book was tantamount to revealing a carnival of faces and masks and the shoddy tricks of authorship. I sat to read an old familiar story but I couldn't recognize the language nor style any longer. It appeared unctuous and repelling. I began to assume that even here lay nothing more than the apocrypha of ghostwriters. I spent the rest of the afternoon examining books once read, their text now entirely new to me.

Stilted or forcibly contrived, they no longer resembled their originals. I marveled at the breadth of this deception unable to grasp its implications in what presently seemed to be the sunset of my life. As I left I heard a rumbling shudder, as though mammoth generators were being turned on.

I hustled back toward my sleeping area in another supernumerary day that had dreamily come to pass. Laying upon the sand, whiling away the evening hours, I gazed like a dog at nothing in particular, wishing for food and a caress.

Awoken by the voices of a few early morning joggers I reflected upon my tired routine. As winter would soon be approaching I began to think of a more suitable shelter and a town that might provide more resources for obtaining food.

Thoughts of a bay that lay to the north began to entertain me. Yes, I happily agreed, why not make my move to a nicer neighborhood, one where it might be easier to distinguish the P.P.A. from this adversity.

The little waves of morning dipped and scuttled, flashing silver in the overcast sky. I could see the cold currents snaking along the watery depths, staking their claims, keeping their distance from the rocks of lands abrupt edge. I lit a cigarette butt I had found in the sand some few feet away. It smelled strangely of grass and manure. I took one more drag then buried it realizing it was marijuana. Suddenly I began to laugh and my appetite bit into me. I slowly packed my belongings and sauntered down a little street with a big smile upon my face. Why I need a cup of coffee, I declared. Or should I say a blup of bloffee, I giggled in portmanteau. And I tottered like a beggar down the road. Intent upon leaving this beach town I made my way toward my northern destination both hungry and thirsty. Soon I came to a restaurant and entered to sit at a counter. I frisked through my pockets for some change I had acquired from telephone booths and pennies from alleyways and curbs that I had scavenged. As I counted I grew astonished at the many shiny denominations it took to buy a simple cup of coffee. It was nice though sitting among

people for a change. Perhaps, after drinking a few cups I might even be able to sneak off with a napkin of leftovers. I was drinking my iced water and coffee when I felt my eyelids dampen and become heavy. An employee came out with a mop and pail of some thickly-scented floor detergent. The air began to fill my nostrils with this cloying candied smell. I heard a soft voice arise with some tenderness. They simply said, with some apology it would seem, that they had run out of plans for me and it was time for me to go. They continued saying that I must breathe deeply, that it would soon be over. I sat there in a trance, yielding to the sentence of my death with quiet resignation.

Filling my lungs with this hemlock, I lay down my head. Not really surprised by my easy surrender, I prepared to fall asleep forever. I heard the table next to me utter something about ultrasound but in my stupor I couldn't distinguish what. Time went by and I obediently inhaled more deeply but I couldn't lose consciousness. I looked down the row of stools and with drowsy eyes I began to focus on my brother.

Again, he was in ample disguise but, nevertheless, recognizable to me. He touched the lobe of his ear to acknowledge me. With haste I lay down my change and rushed passed him muttering 'they're on to you.' I could hear him turn to guardedly say, 'I don't know what you're talking about.' His voice sounded different, almost drugged, and he was, no doubt, put off by this attention I had drawn to him. And I began to reflect back upon my travels wondering if, indeed, everybody was not drugged in one way or another in answering my questions. I paced nervously around the parking lot feeling cowardice and worried about the heroics of my big brother. As I didn't wish to expose him any further I raced off. After marching four or five miles my anxious mind began to slow down and my worry dissipate. I was brightening toward the happy expectations of my new home – the bay! To the song of birds I followed an avenue that flowed like a river with its embankments of large homes. But as I traveled along through this funnel things began to speed up. As an ominous- looking limousine passed by slowly, almost thoughtfully, grave suspicions assaulted me. Once again, as always, the hustle of traffic made preparations for my knightly sojourn. Like the underground in some war-torn, occupied land something tormented and oppressed lay beneath the surface. Who, I wondered, was behind the secret, darkened windows of this coach; the P.P.A. or the devils? I questioned. Oh well,

I thought, chewing on a piece of grass, at least the faces will be different. I stood in front of a motel eying a decanter of coffee in the lobby. The roweled reflection of the sun in the window beamed like a tiger's eye. Thirsty and hungry I took a swallow from my water bottle. It left an acrid taste from the wad of paper I used as a stopper. After some time of forming a plan and summoning my waning courage I strolled in to inquire about any vacancy and the cost of a room for two. I had switched the ring on my hand to the wedding finger and turned its gem inward revealing only a gold band. I proceeded to tell the clerk of my plans to meet my wife here in some few days. I had just returned from Europe visiting my wife's relatives and had arrived here as part of a less expensive charter arrangement, anxiously explained. Though I was, of course, frightened by the web I was spinning when he knew all along who I was, the gentleman that stood to my side distracted from my trust. So, for appearance sake, I resumed my story, fabricating an imaginary reservation date as I moved matter-of-factly toward the coffee. I poured myself a cup, looking quite worldly, I thought, as the clerk busied himself with the reservation calendar. Next I took out my wallet as if to give him a credit card to insure my reservation then I stopped shy, balking with a sigh. No, I told him, it would be wise for me to first approve these dates with my wife, I stuttered. Leaving in a thoughtful way, yawning as if I had jet lag, I told him thank you for your trouble and dismissed myself. Outside I began to shake with some diffidence over the lengths of this inquiry realizing that I hadn't spoken so much another in months. At the seaside boulevard I could hear the waves crashing. Roller skaters, families, and youth clogged my path from freely walking. I became a little agitated over these superfluous troops and shambled toward the water, head bowed. Sitting upon the shore the thunder of the surf began to unnerve me. A field of riotous voices emerged, rubbing their hind legs, so to speak, and machinating with mischief. I sprang to my feet and walked briskly to the arms of the bay. My object was to seek out some refuge where water didn't so formidably conspire with this mob of voices. My blood is still warm, my interlocutors, I protested under my breath. After relieving myself at a public restroom, I noticed a bathing suit hanging to dry upon a brick wall. I slowly looked around. Its owner seemed to be nowhere in sight. Probably it was only a forgotten article or the P.P.A. had left it there for me. As my trunks had been torn all the way up both legs, I looked around one last time. Scoffing at this game I quickly stuffed them into my pack and strolled off happy with my new find. At the bay everything subsided into a desert calm. The storm of activity, both human and natural, seemed to entirely disappear. 'Yes, this was my home,' I cried. Most of the houses were unoccupied it seemed and only a few stragglers and families softly grazed the beach. One large hotel was the only business and, after my inspection, I realized it was nothing more than a resort for a few families. Naturally, there was a cluster of the P.P.A. watching my movements, however, all in all it was the most serene atmosphere I'd experienced since the chase had begun. Evidently the P.P.A. was coming to terms with my foe.

Perhaps they were flexing their muscles at the request of this more affluent neighborhood, I imagined.

My body relaxed and I stretched out in the sand moaning from this relief. No more traffic of people and cars, no businesses nor phone booths, nor car telephones. No more alarms and horns, screams and raucous voices. No more high winds or raging breakwater. No police, no fire trucks, no ambulances, no helicopters nor planes, no jet skies or motorboats. No more computer games, televisions, music. sirens, trains, lawnmowers, leaf blowers, pagers, vacuum cleaners, fans, humming refrigerators, nor cracking walls or ceilings. And no limousines, hoodlums, barkers, two-way radios, nor awkward confrontations. By a large planter, looking into an empty bay I lay down by this seamark and dozed off, pleased with the lullaby of my new residence.

The next morning I awoke at dawn, my thoughts broadcast softly upon the horizon. I sat for a while silent and at peace, sans peur et sans reprocher. I changed into my new swimming trunks and bathed in the cool bay. Submerged I could continue to hear communications hard at work. Not really surprised at this, water being such a fine conductor of sound,

I accepted my lot amicably and swam cherishing the muffled quiet. My heart beat to this waterwheel and the star of the sun pointed into my numb forehead, in this great supernal silence.

Everything visible now seemed no less than truth burning in a dream.

After having luxuriated in the sweet sunlight of my abandoned island into the early afternoon, my stomach began to ache for nourishment. I packed up and tramped downtown. By the time I reached a food stall my mood had swung around. People milled about seemingly without purpose or direction. Empty and saddled, I suppose, with the heavy burden of bidding their time, watching over me.

I rummaged through the garbage hoping to find some remnants of food.

Shortly thereafter, I found a piece of bruised fruit and a part of a sandwich. The coldness of the food made me think uncomfortably of a stranger's spittle. But after crossing this barrier the food began to coat my stomach and I started to feel much better. The coastal boulevard was becoming quite busy and its harsh sound painfully skewered my thoughts. In the distance I could make out the whopping tremors of voices along the water's back. I began to race from this tridents whip, the sirens screaming about me. Dotting my route, more idlers began to assume their positions. Cars stopped, right and left, to dislodge these watchdogs strategically about me. Ibegan to miss my island with each passing moment.

Upon a grassy summit overlooking the ocean I stopped to take stock of things. An older car approached and two men released themselves from its hull they were toting metal detectors and brandishing cigars. As one of them approached I began to sense another foul confrontation. After casual greetings, one of them sat down beside me and my presentiment soon became justified.

He began to talk in a rather desultory fashion. He brought up one thing after another, and I easily perceived that they were no less than instrumental facts surrounding my ordeal. He said, for instance, very smugly, I swear that he smoked cigars as a recourse to seeing a psychiatrist. My body became tense as I listenesd to this dolt pouring over some of the main ingredients of my plight. No doubt, he was trying to nudge my sensibilities by loosely passing through the course of my life. Just like the loon in the café he was caricaturing my meeting with a psychiatrist, making a mockery of me, and so on. Well, I refused to rub elbows with this charlatan and could finally brook no more of this saccharine portrait. I gave him a parting look of omniscience and walked off smirking to myself. After having traveled a few blocks I began to wonder about the true nature of this metal detector. I began to suspect that it was the implement responsible for my doom. I picked up the pace of my walk to the outrage this possibility produced, remembering my many seizures and that singular voice, 'they're killing you with ultrasound. I finally caught sight of the bay and rushed to its safety, swearing off anymore discourse with strangers. For even though myinterpretations might be a little askew this deceit and its revulsion were without words.

IV

Perhaps a month of dreamy languor and solitude dimly passed. I couldn't be sure. The exuberance of the afternoon sun had me pacing to and fro and more than necessary visiting the bustling world on the other side. If it wasn't my isolation driving me out to see if things had somehow changed, then it was my hunger pulling me inside-out. I began to feel more like a prisoner who, having disdained of his private paradise, ran nails into his palms for amusement. As my mind chattered throughout the day it was impossible for me to take refuge from within. S.L.P.S., I would moan. My adversaries knew their business, to be sure. What good was it if this island was nothing more than my doom, my graveyard, my final resting place.

How many days and nights gagged, muzzled, and speechless from the taunting and caprice of these perpetual maledictions did I storm the streets with a heavy heart. My object? To spare the wholesale slaughter of every civil constraint left within me. Thus I was saved more than once or twice by simple perambulation alone from the bent, rusty fan of noise shimmering from the heavens above. The selfsame curses that rendered me an inmate of sorts, expelled me unforgivably and forever from the cozy nest of mankind, and drove the last sanctuary of my mind into an ineluctable form of negation. Each moment I was reborn with the same hideous birth defect. It was always the performance of the sick rat 'they' had by now made of me.

But alas, having acted with the best possible intentions I was beginning to feel the end near. The devouring sea was coming to collect me.I searched through the garbage of a concession stand. A woman from the adjacent restaurant came to me with the remainders of her lunch and a few dollars. I muttered 'thank you,' having to force a twisted, desperate smile. I sat down on the sea wall and polished off this heavy repast, a steak, with my bottle of water. Smothered with introspection and vigilance, insulated to perfection by the medications sprinkled upon my meal, I forged ahead. A rich man I cried to myself. No need to scrounge the rest of the day. I walked to a patio bar where I could sit as if I was a part of humanity. I ordered a coffee and iced water. I was puffing on a cigarette butt, counting my lucky stars, when a clicking sensation appeared in my throat. Mumbling my speeding thoughts now as if forced by reflex, possessed by this strange mental hiccoughing induced by the S.L.P.S., my vocal cords seemed to quiver. I felt like a mockingbird spewing out all of the impressions that had come to me during the day. The underworld began asking me questions concerning the names and whereabouts of friends and family. I fastened onto the television dialogue for the purpose of an easy sabotage, not wanting to drift into their interrogations. 'Small craft advisory, small craft advisory,' I repeated, feeling my voice box was about to burst. My thoughts had turned into small utterances rebounding against the walls , exposing every aspect to their inquiries as if my life was no more than a carnival mirror for public amusement. Abused by this method of superhuman mockery I rushed out babbling and accelerated my pace to escape from the evil range of this mechanism. I was no more than a marionette trying to escape the tough fishing line of their hook.

I dashed through the alleyways trying to hide from the eyes of all others, my head down. My mind jabbered away trying to cover up the contents of my mind with dissimulation. With pulverizing speed, incomprehensible except to the privileged faculties of the S.L.P.S. I fought with all the focus and subterfuge I could possibly muster. Their inquiries continued to press me hard with a vengeance. Never quite able to elude the truth as it necessarily passed before my mind's eye. It was, in fact, impossible. 'They' were, after all, inside me now! The only chance I had was to ramble recklessly like a madman, losing all focus, spitting and raging and fuming incomprehensibly.After a few miles of this uncanny torture I could hear a sonorous clicking noise as if I had finally eluded their range. I continued to walk beneath the sanctuary of shady avenues avoiding the writhing sunlight and 'their' scrambling sensors. I sat down upon a curb, forehead in hands, aggrieved by these trespassers. My mind was gutted out by their exploits and plundering. Suddenly I had an idea. 'Alright,' I wailed inside, 'if I am but this opened diary, a prisoner of war, I will look the part.' I picked myself up and fled to the nearest public restroom. I lathered my head generously with soap, found my razor, and began to shave my head. The water was cold and it took some time but I finally managed. I looked into the mirror, happy with my new appearance, one that more nearly matched my worldly condition and state of mind. I packed my things together and headed in the direction of my 'island' more bald than a newborn. I felt rid of this world and became a little excited over this paradoxical expression of both freedom and enslavement.

Back home at my planter I laid out my sleeping bag and crawled in, zipping up not so much from the cold as protection against the onslaughts of the world. Behind me large empty houses were brooding in the absence of their inhabitants. The voices enunciated their syllables as softly as a sleeping child memorizes the alphabet.

There I lay, realizing that in love, as in death, all is forgiven when apropos of no particular holiday or reason fireworks shot up over the horizon. 'Dandelion,' I said with a simper, feeling cozy and protected by providence once again. 'Dandelion,' I hummed, curling up like an abandoned child in fetal position. 'Dandelion,' I whispered in affection for the people that had befriended me and were now entertaining me with this shower of light. 'Sweet dreams, my daring brothers and sisters,' I offered up in thanks, 'we are soul mates,' and I fell abruptly into sleep.

The next morning I stood within the looping chorale rings of vibration, trembling by a telephone booth. With final resolve, I picked up the receiver and nervously dialed the number. I imagined a thousand false personages, addresses, and phone numbers to throw off the shackles of the S.L.P.S. I heard my friend answer, as from a different world. I told him quickly and summarily of my desire to be taken to a hospital, my location, and a rendezvous time. In between each word, each phrase, that I was by now stammering, I weaved a fine network of dissimulating thought. I hung up and walked to the public restroom. I washed my face, startled at once by the bald stranger in the metal mirror, peering out at me like a prisoner. I took out my toothbrush and put it into my pocket with my passport and threw my sleeping bag and my pack filled with dirty laundry into the trash. Then I walked out, wishing safety for my dear friend, ready for any twisted contingency, glad to be rid of my belongings. Sitting in the dreamy hush, as if after a storm, I began to imagine a new life for myself, wondering if I would ever be able to escape and to forgive the human race for this violent exile from all humanity.

September, 1994
Nipomo, CA

We touch Heaven, when we lay our hands on a human body.

~ Novalis ~

Addendum

Once upon a time.... YES! But why do I feel with such private and undeserved conceit as though somebody somewhere, anywhere, would be the slightest bit interested in reading this little document. I must still be mad! However, at least in a more forgivable way, my being bends with its folly, understanding its threadbare posture, disinherited by next to all. At times I still wonder when they are going to come for me, to disguise and relocate me. I suppose that deep down I always will.

This is my first book , which I wrote in 1994. Like many writers perhaps, all that I have written since then I wrote in desperation to be heard by someone – anyone. It is not that my story is special but that otherwise I will have to settle for a profound emptiness, an isolation without equal.

The intemperate wind and the liquid eye of the sun are, for the moment, replaced by a typewriter and the soft lens of a candle. I sit exorcising, in the soft breeze, my modern day tragedy with an ancient form of catharsis. I sift my mind for the granules of remembrance, repairing myself in fresh installments, taking long walks down the pepper-tree bridle paths of my youth. Long gone my innocence, as is the citrus, where as boys we wandered carefree and resolute to the blossoms of a sacred scent. The rotund oranges were fat and sweet, slacking our thirst. They fell to earth and became the mulch of childhood memory and the folklore to last a lifetime. The atavism from a small heap of voices helps me limp along.

I tap my pen as one tamps a pipe to the rustling of my not so distant past, lighting the pyres as well as avenging the great deception which was mine, and mine alone.

The whispers of both muse and siren alike are still pious enthusiasts, but faint-hearted and well defined. They merely recline, exposed at last. I sit in the golden hay of sunlight, lunching on the sweet meal of quiet solitude. All sea- ick-ened perception has been bludgeoned and jettisoned to sinking death. I can see myself now always walking, pacing endlessly and tirelessly, like a tramp eking out his existence, groping in the darkness. My only lantern made of sweet memory, of childhood embraces, and the enormity of trifles and smiles that carry us clinging to life.

My ignes fatui no longer rev up their engines nor do I wring my hands with incomprehension. My world is empty of its nameless, faceless predators. The dove's cooing still sounds like lament but no longer intones with whispers so pitilessly bleak. I visit the ocean and the waters, too, have lost their entombing glare. Instead they glitter and spin with a halo of sound to the rhythm of deep healing, washing away my cares, erasing the cruder memories of bygone times.

I thank the powers that be for my deliverance. As any man who has gone over the edge I feel like a prisoner without equal, a convict without premeditation or design, a dispossessed king. I still linger in a trance to this corpse of a stunned self and cautiously await another wave of delusions to engulf me. But this is only natural, I tell myself, and time will heal, as they say. We all, like plants, have to struggle toward the light, don't we? It's our instinct, our survival, our destiny. At least, for the moment, I won't be fooled nor nonplussed by this foreign world. But no, I mustn't go on walkabout again. It will be the end of me.

No matter…soon now, they will come in from the fields, these whispering imps. One by one, as mysteriously bidden; barefoot, lame, and dreamy-eyed, they will wind up the creaking staircase. Each with a paraffin lamp and their wicker baskets from a diminished harvest. Each visitant with their given task and modulation, placing their scripts gingerly upon the mantle. Each to return, tentatively, to the nestlings of their fold, as their candles gutter out. Only after their bedtime, I alone, will tend, like the shoemaker to his craft, winding down the clock to face, at long last, the great-soul of silence.

~

Made in United States
Orlando, FL
04 November 2026

90205462R20194